The Music of the Gospel

The Music of the Gospel

Selected Psalms and Inspired Songs of the Bible

by

J.R. Dickens

The Music of the Gospel:
Selected Psalms and Inspired Songs of the Bible

Cover design by J.R. Dickens using Kindle Direct Publishing graphics and templates.

ISBN (paperback): 978-0-9992870-4-0

Printed in the United States of America.

Table of Contents

Acknowledgements

I would like to express my thanks and appreciation to those who have made it possible for me to take part in the ministry of the saints at Winslow Court Senior Living in Colorado Springs:

- Professor Mark House at New Geneva Theological Seminary, who invited me to join the preaching rotation at Winslow Court in the fall of 2022.

- Pastor Matt Holst, elder John Leaf, and elder Ron Marten, at High Plains Fellowship (PCA) in Falcon, Colorado, who encouraged me to try my hand at chapel preaching.

- As well, the provisional leadership that now oversees High Plains Fellowship: Dr. Dominic Aquila, President of New Geneva Theological Seminary; Randy Gray, elder at Covenant Reformed Presbyterian Church (PCA) in Pueblo, Colorado; and Jim Franks, elder at Cheyenne Mountain Presbyterian Church (PCA) in Colorado Springs.

Introduction

The following messages were delivered as part of the chapel ministry at Winslow Court Senior Living in Colorado Springs, Colorado.

I was invited to take part in this ministry by its coordinator, Professor Mark House of New Geneva Theological Seminary. He had a gap to fill in the preaching rotation, and I was a volunteer librarian at the seminary—which is to say, I was close at hand (in this case, literally standing in his office). After conferring with my church's leadership, I was given the green light.

There's a little more to the story, of course, but that's the short version. I've now been helping at Winslow Court for more than a year.

I chose the book of Psalms as a starting point—with the intent that each message would be essentially self-contained so that whoever was listening, on whichever occasion, would profit from the message. I have allowed my own curiosity to be the basis for starting with Psalm 49 and for selecting the psalms that have followed afterward. While there is not a "master plan," you'll see that I've been gravitating toward psalms that are frequently quoted in the New Testament.

The ministry at Winslow Court has proven to be a new challenge for someone who has been teaching in the church for many years now. Since this is my first experiment in preaching, I have tried to "keep it simple"—sticking close to the biblical text, explaining what it means, making some applications, and tying it up with the gospel.

There are some patterns that naturally emerge from the following messages—the most important of which is the finished work of Christ—that he has accomplished everything necessary for salvation and that he rules and reigns from heaven. Corollaries includes the warning that man's efforts at salvation (or anything else) are futile apart from God—that man cannot work his way into God's favor, and he cannot pay the price of his own soul; that God makes a difference between those who receive his mercy ("lovingkindness"—*hesed*) and those who receive his justice; that the righteous will suffer persecution—and even death—at the hands of the wicked, but that God promises to deliver his saints from all their temporal hardships; that we must not put our trust in earthly princes, but only in the Prince who reigns from the heavenly city of Zion. In the psalms there is a promise of a place where righteousness reigns forever, and the saints will have a share in that kingdom. In the meantime, the psalms also warn that man in his Fall is far worse than we want to admit: that apart from the regenerating grace of God, man is capable of unimaginable brutality. Many such doctrines are clearly set down in the psalms, and even though they are wrapped in poetic language, they are often clarified and reinforced by their use in the New Testament. And the frequent use of the psalms in the New Testament is a demonstration of the perfect continuity of scripture from start to finish. Man is to live by every word that comes from the mouth of God (Deut 8:3, quoted by Jesus in Matt 4:4).

I hope you will find these messages edifying and encouraging—that you may be strengthened in your love of God's word, and the love of his Son Jesus.

Some editorial boilerplate now follows.

While sermons may involve considerable scholarship behind the scenes, they are not necessarily intended to be scholarly works—they are designed, first of all, to edify a congregation of believers and to challenge any unbelievers in the audience to put their faith in Christ. Consequently, the citations are minimal and are generally directed at the biblical text itself. Many commentators are mentioned and directly quoted, but the citations are selective. In some cases, comments are quoted from secondary contributors, as in *The Treasury of David*, where Spurgeon compiled quotations from hundreds of individual contributors. The Bibliography will make it possible to track down those details for the curious reader.

Biblical quotations from the *Legacy Standard Bible* (LSB) retain the capitalization for Old Testament quotations in the New Testament. Any italics in the original biblical text have been removed from the offset quotations. Where italics now appear, it is for the author's emphasis. Throughout these messages, biblical paraphrases and fragments are italicized but are not specifically footnoted. The author is assuming a modicum of literary license, as well as a modicum of biblical literacy on the part of the reader.

Finally, the source text of this book proceeds from the "closed caption" AI transcriptions of the recordings posted on SermonAudio, over which the author retains copyright ownership. The messages contained here are only lightly edited and reflect the original speech with considerable accuracy. I have only touched up a few defects and inserted some helpful footnotes. Consequently, the style reflects the way I *speak*, not the way I *write*. The AI transcription algorithm, frankly, has some difficulty figuring out how to punctuate my free-stream speech with its frequent run-on sentences. So I beg pardon for the grammatical shortcomings, if that proves to be tedious to the reader.

The Price of a Soul (Psalm 49)

November 27, 2022

The passage that we're going to be looking at today is from the Psalter—Psalm 49. I have chosen a new translation to use for the time that we have together in the psalms, for reasons that will become more apparent perhaps a little later on, not so much today. But it's called the *Legacy Standard Bible* (LSB), and it's in the tradition of the *New American Standard Bible* (NASB). It is seeking to provide for us a very literal and a very accurate translation from the original languages. So I'll be reading from the *Legacy Standard Bible* version of Psalm 49, and read along with me if you have that, otherwise give it your attention.

1 Hear this, all peoples;
Give ear, all inhabitants of the world,
2 Both low and high,
Rich and poor together.
3 My mouth will speak wisdom,
And the meditation of my heart will be discernment.
4 I will incline my ear to a proverb;
I will express my riddle on the harp.

5 Why should I fear in days of evil,
When the iniquity of my supplanters surrounds me,
6 Even those who trust in their wealth
And boast in the abundance of their riches?
7 Truly, no man can redeem his brother;
He cannot give to God a ransom for him—
8 For the redemption price for their soul is costly,
And it ceases forever—

9 That he should live on eternally,
That he should not see corruption.

10 For he sees that even wise men die;
The fool and the senseless alike perish
And leave their wealth to others.
11 Their inner thought is that their houses are forever
And their dwelling places from generation to generation;
They have called their lands after their own names.
12 But man in his honor will not endure;
He is like the animals that perish.

13 This is the way of those who are foolish,
And of those after them who are pleased with their words.
Selah.
14 As sheep they are appointed for Sheol;
Death will shepherd them;
And the upright shall have dominion over them in the morning,
And their form shall be for Sheol to consume,
Far away from his habitation.
15 But God will redeem my soul from the power of Sheol,
For He will receive me. Selah.

16 Do not be afraid when a man becomes rich,
When the glory of his house increases;
17 For when he dies he will not take any of it;
His glory will not descend after him.
18 For while he lives he blesses his soul—
And men will praise you when you do well for yourself—
19 But his soul shall go to the generation of his fathers;
They will eternally not see light.

20 Man in his honor, but who does not understand,
Is like the animals that perish.[1]

The message title that I want to use for today is *The Price of a Soul*. And we'll start with a little bit of background on this particular psalm. You might notice that it's unusual, and we want to think about why this is an unusual psalm. In the first place—a little boilerplate—we're not really sure who wrote it or when, or whether there was a particular occasion for it to be written. And one of the things that makes this an unusual psalm is that it's not a prayer *per se*. We tend to think of the psalms as being prayers, and yet this is not a prayer. It is actually a call for wisdom. The psalmist is calling for us to pay attention to his words. And as such, God is not addressed by this psalm. He's mentioned, but God is not the object of the psalmist's words in the psalm. We notice that it is a universal call. And that also makes it interesting—because God's word is not just for God's people. God's word is for *all* people. And here's a case where God's word is very explicitly calling *everyone* to pay attention, to listen up. So it's a call to all men everywhere. And we can add to that, not only all men everywhere, but for all time. Part of what makes it an unusual psalm is that it doesn't matter where you may place it in the course of history,

[1] Psalm 49 (LSB). Quoted again afterward.

but it applies equally well whether we go as far back in history as we can, or whether we bring it to the very present day.

So it's talking about a universal problem. It's a universal condition. And that condition is inequality. It's something that we hear a lot about these days. And there are those who want to use a great deal of force, by the way, to try to make everyone equal. And yet, that becomes a futile exercise. So that's the problem that it's addressing, and not just the problem of inequality *per se*, but the problems that come from that.

In terms of structure, this psalm is divided into five stanzas. We'll look at the main point in each of those five stanzas. So we'll just follow it through as it's written. Each of those stanzas has three to five verses. As a poem, we should notice that its literary structure is in repetitive *couplets*. This is a very typical use of Hebrew poetry, where you have a verse that says two things, the same, just slightly differently. And when we see those kinds of repetitions, the idea is that this is something important that we want to make sure that we pay attention to. So that is how Hebrew poetry provides emphasis where today we might use boldface or underline or all caps and those kinds of things—as if to say, this is important, let's pay attention to it. So that gives us a starting point for understanding a little about this psalm.

As we start to look at the text, what I want you to notice—again in very typical fashion for the psalms and for Proverbs—there are very, very strong contrasts, extremes. We're going as far to the extremes as we can in describing what's happening. And here the extremes are between the rich and the poor. And it's not their riches or their poverty that makes them extreme. It's the condition of their souls. And that's what we're primarily going to be concerned about here today.

The first four verses that we'll look at, we can call this stanza, *a call to listen up*.

> 1 Hear this, all peoples;
> Give ear, all inhabitants of the world,
> 2 Both low and high,
> Rich and poor together.
> 3 My mouth will speak wisdom,
> And the meditation of my heart will be discernment.
> 4 I will incline my ear to a proverb;
> I will express my riddle on the harp.

And as I read those verses, hopefully you can see what I mean by the repetitive nature of these verses. *Hear this all peoples, give ear all inhabitants*. Those kinds of patterns continue throughout the psalm. So who is the psalm is speaking to? I think we've got that answer, don't we? Everybody, everybody. No one is excluded from this. What is it that the psalmist wants to say? He says that he wants to speak wisdom and discernment. And he's going to speak it in terms of a proverb or a riddle. And what we don't see in the English translation, by the way, is that those words, *wisdom*, *discernment*, *understanding*, are actually plural words. It would be a little awkward to say *wisdoms* or *understandings* or *discernments*. But again, the plural nature of those words is emphasizing the importance of it. How's the psalmist going to do this? He says he's going to do it on his harp with a song. And what's significant about a song? It's meant to be remembered. It's easier for us to remember songs than it is for us to remember simple prose.

Now we begin to get into the issue and we can ask this question: who is it who makes rich and poor, low and high? And again, those are inclusive statements so that there's literally no one who is excluded from that call: rich *and* poor, low *and* high. One of the ways that we see this is in 1 Samuel. And you'll recall in 1 Samuel, Hannah is childless and she's praying for a son who's going to be named Samuel. And in her prayer, she says this:

> 6 "Yahweh puts to death and makes alive;
> He brings down to Sheol and raises up.
> 7 "Yahweh makes poor and rich;
> He brings low; He also exalts.
> 8 "He raises the poor from the dust;
> He exalts the needy from the ash heap
> To make them sit with nobles,
> And inherit a seat of glory;

> For the pillars of the earth are Yahweh's,
> And He set the world on them."[2]

So when we notice the inequality between people, we need to be reminded that it's actually God who gives or removes. We think of the story of Job and how he was one of the richest men of his day. And yet in a series of calamities, he lost essentially everything that he had, including his own family. So we need to have that in mind—that God in his providence determines who has what. And we'll see that part of our response should be that we are content with what we have. We'll talk a little more about that in a moment. For now we recognize that as God who makes both poor and rich, low and high, whoever might be exalted, in office or in power, or whoever might be lowly, that God has determined our places.

Next, let's ask, as we start this study, what is wisdom? What does he mean when he says wisdom? Where does it come from? And what is it worth? And here's where the book of Proverbs will help us fill in the answer to those kinds of questions. I'm going to look at a portion of chapter three in Proverbs, starting in verse 13.

> 13 How blessed is the man who finds wisdom
> And the man who obtains discernment.

---

[2] 1 Sam 2:6-8 (LSB)

And listen to this, for *her profit*—wisdom—is personified in this passage.

14 For her profit is better than the profit of silver
And her produce better than fine gold.
15 She is more precious than pearls;
And nothing you desire compares with her.
16 Length of days is in her right hand;
In her left hand are riches and glory.
17 Her ways are pleasant ways
And all her pathways are peace.
18 She is a tree of life to those who seize her,
And all those who hold her fast are blessed.

And if we're still wondering where wisdom is coming from, look at verse 19:

19 Yahweh by wisdom founded the earth,
By discernment He established the heavens.
20 By His knowledge the deeps were split up
And the skies drip with dew.

And then it gets more personal:

21 My son, let them not deviate from your eyes;
Guard sound wisdom and discretion,
22 So they will be life for your soul
And grace for your neck.
23 Then you will walk in your way securely
And your foot will not stumble.
24 When you lie down, you will not be in dread;

You will lie down, and your sleep will be pleasant.
25 Do not be afraid of sudden dread
Nor of the storm of the wicked when it comes;
26 For Yahweh will be your confidence
And will keep your foot from being caught.
27 Do not withhold good from those to whom it is due,
When it is in your hand to do it.[3]

Something that's remarkable about Proverbs in these opening chapters is how wisdom is personified. It's not just a thing or an idea, but is of such importance that we can even describe it in personal terms. Wisdom comes from the Lord, the Lord who is the source of all wisdom, the one who founded the earth by wisdom and by understanding. And so this wisdom that we're referring to as a supernatural wisdom is not something that you're going to find by going and looking from place to place here on earth. But wisdom is found in the word of God, which is what we're looking at right now.

What is this wisdom worth? And the answer is, pick the most valuable earthly treasures that you can think of, and it's worth *more* than that. Because there's nothing of earthly treasures that can be used either to put a value on wisdom, or to buy it. And that's what we're going to be looking at here in Psalm 49.

[3] Prov 3:13-27 (LSB)

The next few verses I've titled, *no ransom is enough.*

5 Why should I fear in days of evil,
When the iniquity of my supplanters surrounds me,
6 Even those who trust in their wealth
And boast in the abundance of their riches?
7 Truly, no man can redeem his brother;
He cannot give to God a ransom for him—
8 For the redemption price for their soul is costly,
And it ceases forever—

Or if you like, *it's never sufficient.*

9 That he should live on eternally,
That he should not see corruption.

So there's a little bit of a lamentation here by the psalmist. He's alluding to the fact that he's living in days of evil. And what is it that typically makes days *evil?* It's usually some suffering that's brought by fellow man. And who are the ones that are typically bringing the suffering? It's the ones that are the rich and the powerful. And so at any time in history, we could say that we have this same kind of problem—that the rich grow rich, sometimes by deception, sometimes by thievery and other sin. And that when they gain their riches and they gain the power that goes with it, they often use that against those who are powerless. But that's not really the theme of this stanza because it starts with the rhetorical question, *why should I fear in days of evil?* He's saying there's no reason to fear in days of evil. Even though he says that he's surrounded by iniquity, he can say that he is without fear. So the universal problem that we're wrestling with is that those who gain in riches are often oppressing the poor with those riches. And that becomes an issue of justice. When the poor are oppressed, they're often crying out for justice. When justice is not seen in this life, those who are oppressed are crying for justice from heaven.

Notice the foolishness here—that those who are rich think that they can buy eternity with their riches. And here's how we could add, that you can't outsmart the grave. Nobody is going to outsmart the grave. No man can ransom another from the grave. He can try as hard as he likes and he cannot do it. And that's a reminder that the money that they have, no matter how much it may be, no matter what riches it may be, no matter how much earthly power they may have, they do not have power over the grave. And we're also mindful that a man's *value* cannot be measured in terms of money. It doesn't matter how much you have. Man is of such surpassing value that nothing of this world's riches is sufficient as a ransom for a man's soul.

This is how William Graham Scroggie has expressed the idea:

> There are two kinds of men: those who make a God of their wealth and those who find their wealth in God.

There's the contrast that I spelled out for you at the beginning—the contrast between those who place their trust in riches and those who place their trust in God. And this is where the great division is going to come.

In the next three verses, we see *the foolish pretention of the rich*. Verse 10:

> 10 For he sees that even wise men die;
> The fool and the senseless alike perish
> And leave their wealth to others.
> 11 Their inner thought is that their houses are forever
> And their dwelling places from generation to generation;
> They have called their lands after their own names.
> 12 But man in his honor will not endure;
> He is like the animals that perish.

And we're going to see this refrain again at the end of the psalm. This idea that the man without understanding—who is relying on his material things—is like a beast, that just like the beast, he's going to perish and be gone. So here we say that death comes to all men. Whatever inequality we may have in this life, equality comes by the grave because everyone goes down to the grave, whether wise or foolish, whether rich or poor.

We notice that this wise or this rich man in his pretention, we could say he has a *Plan A* and a *Plan B*. Plan A is he wants to live forever. He thinks his money and his power can allow him to live forever. But we notice he's also hedging his bets just a little bit. Plan B is if Plan A doesn't work, he's going to leave a legacy. Notice how it says that *they have called their lands after their own names*. And you don't have to drive very far in virtually any town to see names on street signs, or names on monuments, monuments to men who came before, who tried to leave their name on those things. And their names may be familiar and yet their memory is still forgotten in time.

We notice the futility of trusting in your riches because obviously all worldly wealth stays in this world when the rich man dies. As the old expression goes, and it's true, you can't take it with you. And it might be for the better or for the worse, but the fact is that somebody else is going to get it after you're gone. It might be somebody who didn't work for it. As Solomon says in the book of Ecclesiastes, *a man may toil all of his life to build his wealth, and who knows whether the one who comes after him is going to be wise or foolish*. But in any case, whatever we accumulate in this life has to be left behind. They want a legacy that will endure, and yet it fades in time. All earthly honor has to pass away. And again, like the beasts who perish, so too is the man who tries to make a name for himself. This is what Solomon in the book of Ecclesiastes says over and over and over again, when he says, all is *vanity*, *vanity*, *vanity*. What does that mean? *Futility*. It avails nothing in the end.[4]

Now on to the next stanza. We'll call it, *the great divide*. Verse 13:

> 13 This is the way of those who are foolish,
> And of those after them who are pleased with their words. Selah.
> 14 As sheep they are appointed for Sheol;
> Death will shepherd them;
> And the upright shall have dominion over them in the morning,
> And their form shall be for Sheol to consume,
> Far away from his habitation.

And the pause is for what comes next: *but God*.

> 15 But God will redeem my soul from the power of Sheol,
> For He will receive me. Selah.

At the beginning of this psalm, we noticed that it is a universal call to rich and poor alike. And you might say, why do the poor need to know this? Why do the poor need to be told not to trust in their riches because they don't have any riches to trust in? And the answer comes in verse 13:

---

[4] Vanity also carries the idea of fleeting—temporary—things that are vanishing like a mist. See commentaries on Psalm 94 and 127.

those after them who are pleased with their words. What does that mean? Those who desire the things that the rich already have, whether wealth or whether power. And so we ultimately see that whether rich or poor, you may yet be in sin. It can be the sin of pretention for the rich, or the sin of envy for the poor. So the warning has to be universal. The poor man can be just as foolish as the wise man when he envies the one who has riches. And as we said before, if it's the case that God makes men both rich and poor according to his riches, as we saw in Proverbs—everything belongs to God and he gives it to whom he pleases—then there's no cause for us to envy.

There's an odd expression in this part of the psalm, that *death is the shepherd of the foolish* and that *the upright will prevail*. And here we have the picture of sheep as being powerless. And so sheep, the rich sheep as it were, are being shepherded into the grave because they have no power in themselves to resist death. The grave consumes all who go down to the earth, meaning what? We all die and we return to the dust from which we're made.

Now, just how costly is the price of a life? That's the big takeaway that I want you to have today, and it is found in those words, *but God*. Because what is impossible for man is possible for God. And we want to turn briefly to the book of Matthew to look at a couple of verses there, just to emphasize that point so that we hear it from Jesus himself saying this to us. Matthew 19.

When the rich young man comes to see Jesus and says, *what must I do to inherit eternal life?* He goes through the list of the commandments. You need to do this and this and this and this. And his response is what? *I've done all that*. And then Jesus says what? *There's only one thing that you lack. And that is to go and sell everything that you have, give it to the poor, and then come and follow me*. And what is his response? Does he leave joyful? No, he leaves despondent, because why? Jesus exposed the fact that though he had great riches, he was also making those riches an idol for himself. In verse 23:

> And Jesus said to His disciples, "Truly I say to you, it is hard for a rich man to enter the kingdom of heaven. And again I say to you, it is easier for a camel to go through the eye of a needle, than for a rich man to enter the kingdom of God." And when the disciples heard this, they were very astonished and said, "Then who can be saved?" And looking at them Jesus said to them, "With people this is impossible, but with God all things are possible."[5]

The son of man, Jesus, is the one who came to ransom men's souls. And in the very next chapter, we see Jesus saying this:

---

[5] Matt 19:23-26 (LSB)

> ". . . just as the Son of Man did not come to be served, but to serve, and to give His life a ransom for many."[6]

A *ransom* meaning what? A *purchase*. It's only the blood of Christ that has the value that's necessary to purchase the life of a soul. And so we see in the book of Romans, as sin reigns in death, grace reigns in righteousness to eternal life through Jesus Christ, our Lord. Sin brings all men down to the grave. But guess what? Christ went into the grave himself to conquer the power of death. In verse 15 of our psalm, it says, *he will receive me*. And there are those who say it might be better understood that he will *take* me, just as God took Enoch way back in the book of Genesis—that Enoch walked with God and God took him. He didn't die. The idea that it is God who does the taking. Here's how we can put it. That Christ is the grave robber. Sin brings us down to the grave, but Christ goes into the grave and brings us out to give us eternal life.

The last five verses we'll call *living at peace*. Verse 16:

> 16 Do not be afraid when a man becomes rich,
> When the glory of his house increases;
> 17 For when he dies he will not take any of it;
> His glory will not descend after him.

---

[6] Matt 20:28 (LSB)

18 For while he lives he blesses his soul—
And men will praise you when you do well for yourself—
19 But his soul shall go to the generation of his fathers;
They will eternally not see light.
20 Man in his honor, but who does not understand,
Is like the animals that perish.

And here we have in mind that Jesus on several occasions warned those who are pretentious, who are seeking the accolades that come from men, will have their reward in full. In other words, enjoy the praises of men because that's all you get. When the life to come arrives, you will not have a reward, but you will face judgment.

So there's no need for us to fear the rich and the powerful. We're reminded that their lives are merely a mist. We are told specifically, in places like Psalm 37, not to fret about the wicked. And I want to read just a couple of verses of that.

1 Do not fret because of evildoers,
Be not envious toward doers of unrighteousness.
2 For they will wither quickly like the grass
And fade like the green herb.

And what does he say next?

3 Trust in Yahweh and do good;
Dwell in the land and cultivate faithfulness.

4 Delight yourself in Yahweh;
And He will give you the desires of your heart.

5 Commit your way to Yahweh,
Trust in Him, and He will do it.
6 He will bring forth your righteousness as the light
And your judgment as the noonday.[7]

Very same idea expressed just a little more explicitly. Here's the contrast. The man without understanding or wisdom has nothing but the darkness of the grave and an eternity of judgment to see as his future. And again, the refrain is that the man without understanding is like the beasts. He goes down to the grave and he is no more. The man who has wisdom is blessed beyond measure because that wisdom prepares him to meet the grave.

So we'll finish with these exhortations.

First of all, listen, get wisdom, get understanding. And here I would add, don't *wait* for it, *work* for it. And *how* do we do that? We do that by immersing ourselves in the word of God and asking for God's Spirit to guide us into his wisdom.

---

[7] Ps 37:1-6 (LSB)

Next, do not trust in the things of this world because riches cannot save you and whatever you have may vanish in a moment.

Next, do not envy the rich because their life is vanity—futility—and their end is destruction. There's nothing there that you should want to envy.

Next, do not fear the powerful because they will soon pass away and be forgotten. And no matter how much the rich and powerful may rage, remember that the grave puts an end to their raging. Their influence will die with them.

And lastly, trust in the one who ransoms your soul from the grave, who gives riches that last not for a lifetime, but for eternity. Put your trust in Christ. Wisdom is to be found in him as a person and in his word. Immerse yourself in that word.

Let's pray. Father, we thank you for this message today and ask that you would indeed apply it to each of our hearts through your Spirit, that you would give us greater wisdom and understanding, and that you would cause us to seek wisdom and understanding through your word, knowing that it is powerful and effective and accomplishes all that you would have it to do for us now and in eternity, that we may be in your presence and give praises to you at the throne of grace, and unto the Lamb. In Christ's name we pray. Amen.

From Revelation to Redemption (Psalm 19)

December 4, 2022

Our message today comes from the psalms once again. This is Psalm 19, which is a psalm that is somewhat like Psalm 119 in miniature, like a somewhat condensed version of it, where we sense that David is one who truly loves the law of God, and is extolling the law of God, and he's doing it in a very short few verses here in this psalm. I'm going to read again from the *Legacy Standard Bible* (LSB). There are 14 verses here, so please give it your attention as we read.

1 The heavens are telling of the glory of God;
And the expanse is declaring the work of His hands.
2 Day to day pours forth speech,
And night to night reveals knowledge.
3 There is no speech, nor are there words;
Their voice is not heard.
4 Their line has gone out through all the earth,
And their utterances to the end of the world.
In them He has placed a tent for the sun,
5 Which is as a bridegroom coming out of his chamber;
It rejoices as a strong man to run his course.
6 Its rising is from one end of the heavens,
And its circuit to the other end of them;
And there is nothing hidden from its heat.

7 The law of Yahweh is perfect, restoring the soul;
The testimony of Yahweh is sure, making wise the simple.
8 The precepts of Yahweh are right, rejoicing the heart;
The commandment of Yahweh is pure, enlightening the eyes.

9 The fear of Yahweh is clean, enduring forever;
The judgments of Yahweh are true; they are righteous altogether.
10 They are more desirable than gold, even more than much fine gold;
Sweeter also than honey and the drippings of the honeycomb.
11 Moreover, by them Your slave is warned;
In keeping them there is great reward.

12 Who can discern his errors? Acquit me of hidden faults.
13 Also keep back Your slave from presumptuous sins;
Let them not rule over me;
Then I will be blameless,
And I shall be acquitted of great transgression.
14 Let the words of my mouth and the meditation of my heart
Be acceptable in Your sight,
O Yahweh, my rock and my Redeemer.[8]

So let's consider a little background as we get started in this psalm. It's attributed to David's authorship, about 3,000 years ago, which is pretty remarkable when we think about how old some of the scriptures are, and yet how they are timeless. It's obviously a praise psalm for the God who made all things. That's the first portion of the psalm, the extolling of God's *creation*. And then it turns very suddenly to extolling God's *law*. If you follow along in the psalm, you'll notice that it's full of what we could call poetic parallelisms. Remember last time we talked about how, in Hebrew poetry, repetition occurs frequently as what? As a way of

[8] Ps 19 (LSB). Quoted again afterward.

emphasizing the importance of what we're reading. And this psalm is full of that. In fact, there's a very important sixfold repetition regarding God's law that we're going to take a look at.

Something else that we'll see is that this psalm prefigures the gospel, which will reach the ends of the earth. What were we just singing about in our carol? The Sun of righteousness who goes into all the world with the gospel. The big idea for this psalm is that we can see the power of God in his creation, but we need to see in his written law, the character of God. So those two things work together. They're not independent of one another, but the first brings us to the second.

There are three sections in this psalm, which we'll consider in turn. And as I mentioned last time, my particular reason for using the *Legacy Standard Bible*, which is a newer translation, you were able to see when we just read this psalm. How does it render God's name? Instead of *the* LORD, which is what most English translations use, it translates his name as *Yahweh*. And the other thing that you might've picked up on, which might be a little unpleasant to the American ear, is the use of the language of *slaves*, calling himself a *slave* to God. So the LSB is more consistent in the way that it renders both God's covenant name, *Yahweh*, as well as the terms in Hebrew and in Greek that are properly translated as *slave*. And the contrast there is between the slave and his *master*.

Let's take a look at the first six verses. I'll reread this starting in verse one.

1 The heavens are telling of the glory of God;
And the expanse is declaring the work of His hands.
2 Day to day pours forth speech,
And night to night reveals knowledge.
3 There is no speech, nor are there words;
Their voice is not heard.
4 Their line has gone out through all the earth,
And their utterances to the end of the world.
In them He has placed a tent for the sun,
5 Which is as a bridegroom coming out of his chamber;
It rejoices as a strong man to run his course.
6 Its rising is from one end of the heavens,
And its circuit to the other end of them;
And there is nothing hidden from its heat.

So let's do a little detective work. What's being referred to here? The technical term is *natural revelation*. In other words, God is revealing himself through the things that he has made. When did he start doing that? When he started creating, so from the beginning. How long has he been doing that? And the answer is, starting at the beginning of creation and continuing until the end of the world. And what else about this is interesting is that it is both *day* and *night*, in different ways, that it is *never-ending*, and that it's *universal*—meaning that everybody in every language can understand the existence and the power of God by looking at what has been made. So there are no excuses. Now there's figurative language, of course—this is poetic literature, so we're not surprised to find some figurative language and metaphorical language—but we understand the point, don't we?

In these first few verses, interestingly, the first mention of God is using what is considered the most generic name for him in the Hebrew language, and that is *El*, very generic. What we're going to see in this next passage is that the transition of the psalmist is to start referring to him by his personal covenant name. So we know God in the most general sense from these first few verses from his creation. God as Creator is a recurring theme in scripture. It comes up over and over and over again. It's one of the reasons why I'm such a strong defender of literal six-day creation because he keeps bringing creation up over and over and over again as if our understanding of creation is important to understanding him and his work. The sad thing is that the modern man, because of his belief in science, he rejects both God as the Creator and the law that God has given to us. So we would put it like this: natural revelation is one of the ways that God reveals himself to us, but we need something more. He reveals his existence and his power, but we need to know more in order to know how to be saved. So this is where his written word comes in, and particularly the law.

This idea of *the line going out* could indicate a couple of different things, but we'll see in a moment that that verse is quoted by the apostle Paul in the book of Romans. And interestingly, when he's referring to it there, it talks about *words*. There is a sense in which the creation is speaking forth in a way that every man can understand. Now about this creation, lights are made in the very beginning to mark the times and the seasons. Let me quote momentarily from Genesis chapter one, verses 14 and 15, on the fourth day when God said:

> "Let there be lights in the expanse of the heavens to separate the day from the night, and let them be for signs and for seasons and for days and years; and let them be for lights in the expanse of the heavens to give light on the earth"; and it was so.[9]

And so what's interesting, as we examine this creation, we notice these things, that the sun marks the days, day by day. The moon marks the months, month by month. And the stars also have a purpose in this calendar, which is to mark the years. This is a particularly favorite time of the year for me in part because the constellation that I'm most familiar with starts to appear in the eastern sky at this time of the year. It's the constellation Orion. And interestingly, it's one of several constellations that are specifically mentioned in scripture.

---

[9] Gen 1:14-15 (LSB).

Now, first we notice about the stars, that *he calls them all by name*. This is a quote from Isaiah chapter 40 and verse 26, where he says:

> Lift up your eyes on high
> And see who has created these stars,
> The One who leads forth their host by number,
> He calls them all by name;
> Because of the greatness of His vigor and the strength of His power,
> Not one of them is missing.[10]

All those stars, that try as they might, our scientists cannot number. God has numbered and named every one of them. There are two stars in particular that are very visible in the constellation Orion. One is called Betelgeuse. It's the right shoulder of Orion the Hunter. The other one is called Rigel and it's his left leg. And those stars, which are mere points of light to us in the night sky, are massive, unfathomably massive. Our astronomers tell us that Rigel is about 80 times the diameter of our own sun, and that Betelgeuse is about 800 times the diameter of our own sun. And we'll come back to the question of why is it that God creates these fantastic parts of his creation, things that we can scarcely imagine. And by the way, these stars are so far away that if we could travel at the speed of light, it would take us at least 600 years to get to the closer one, and it would take us nearly 900 to get to the other one, at the speed of light, if

[10] Is 40:26 (LSB).

you can imagine. And the funny thing is that in the scheme of this universe that God has made, those stars are actually pretty close by. They're not that far away as cosmological distance goes.

So what we know about that creation, it ought to drive us to the one who created it. We ought to have a sense of the power and the majesty of God on the basis of what he has created. So creation is a constant witness. Man cannot deny it and he cannot silence it. We notice at times how hard man tries to silence the word of God, but he cannot silence the cosmos. So we have both creation as well as conscience that testify to the existence of God. Man cannot escape his own moral nature. He knows that he has a moral nature and he knows that he is guilty before his Creator.

Charles Spurgeon puts it like this:

> He who looks up to the firmament and then writes himself down an atheist, brands himself at the same moment as an idiot and a liar.

It's a moral problem when we reject the existence of God because he has revealed himself so clearly through what has been made. Here's what we see—that when man begins to ponder God's creation, we're going to find that he will either turn his heart *upward* toward God, or he'll turn it *downward* toward the creation. And here's where Paul, in the first chapter of the book of Romans, explains what happens when man tries to reject the existence of God. I'm in chapter one, starting in verse 20.

> For since the creation of the world His invisible attributes, both His eternal power and divine nature, have been clearly seen, being understood through what has been made, so that they are without excuse. For even though they knew God, they did not glorify Him as God or give thanks, but they became futile in their thoughts, and their foolish heart was darkened. Professing to be wise, they became fools, and exchanged the glory of the incorruptible God for an image in the likeness of corruptible man and of birds and four-footed animals and crawling creatures.
>
> Therefore God gave them over in the lusts of their hearts to impurity, so that their bodies would be dishonored among them. For they exchanged the truth of God for a lie, and worshiped and served the creature rather than the Creator, who is blessed forever. Amen.[11]

That's the indictment against man. In his fallenness, he looks at the glory of the creation and says, *there is no God*. Now, the funny thing is that nature, as God made it, is the reality in which we all have to live. And again, that ought to compel us to turn toward our Creator rather than trying to live against the creation as he's made it. Unfortunately, it's the case, as scripture says, that fallen man is under a powerful delusion. He

[11] Rom 1:20-25 (LSB).

convinces himself that there is no God, and why? So that he can escape the consequences of the law, which is what we're going to be looking at next. It's a sad fact that man has allowed his belief in the power of nature, so-called, to displace God from his thoughts. And I think it's fair to say that man can't and shouldn't be bothered to meditate upon a universe if it was all just chance. Why would you bother? Meanwhile, David is showing us in the psalm what our response *ought* to be: praise for the one who created all things. It's also the case that the heavens ought to show man just how small he is and how little he controls. Think about it this way. Could man stop that sun from rising from his tabernacle each day and running his course? *Nope*. Could he resist the one who *made* the sun? *No*. And then we're reminded of a conversation that God had with Job when he asked him a couple of specific questions. *Can you bind the Pleiades or can you lose the belt of Orion?* And what's the obvious answer? Man has no such power. So the revelation of God that we see in nature should drive us to the law of God. And again, this idea of *the sun running its course* and *the bridegroom coming forth* can be understood as allusions to Christ. And we'll see just why that is when we look at how this verse is used in the book of Romans.

This is what we read in Romans 10. And I'll start in verse 14.[12] Here, Paul is asking the question about the preaching of the gospel and the importance of the gospel reaching the ends of the earth, every corner.

> How then will they call on Him in whom they have not believed? How will they believe in Him whom they have not heard? And how will they hear without a preacher? And how will they preach unless they are sent? Just as it is written, "HOW BEAUTIFUL ARE THE FEET OF THOSE WHO PROCLAIM GOOD NEWS OF GOOD THINGS!"
>
> However, they did not all heed the good news, for Isaiah says, "LORD, WHO HAS BELIEVED OUR REPORT?" So faith comes from hearing, and hearing by the word of Christ.
>
> But I say, have they never heard? On the contrary, they have; . . .

And here's where he quotes the psalm.

> "THEIR VOICE HAS GONE OUT INTO ALL THE EARTH, AND THEIR WORDS TO THE ENDS OF THE WORLD."

So just as the sun brings light every place it goes, so also does the gospel.

---

[12] Capitalization is used in the LSB text to indicate quotations from the Old Testament in the New Testament.

Let's consider the next few verses, starting in verse seven. Now the psalmist turns his attention to the law. And listen to the repetition as I read these verses. Listen to how many different ways the law is referred to. It's going to be *referred to*, it's going to be given a term to *describe* it, and it's also going to be given an *effect*. So listen to what the law *is* and what it *does*.

> 7 The law of Yahweh is perfect, restoring the soul;
> The testimony of Yahweh is sure, making wise the simple.
> 8 The precepts of Yahweh are right, rejoicing the heart;
> The commandment of Yahweh is pure, enlightening the eyes.
> 9 The fear of Yahweh is clean, enduring forever;
> The judgments of Yahweh are true; they are righteous altogether.
> 10 They are more desirable than gold, even more than much fine gold;
> Sweeter also than honey and the drippings of the honeycomb.
> 11 Moreover, by them Your slave is warned;
> In keeping them there is great reward.

This brings us to what's called the *second book*. The first is *the book of nature* where God reveals himself through his creation. And now we come to *the book of the law*, the book of revelation. And we have that written revelation in the form of our Bible. So again, if we want to know whether God exists, we can see that in nature. If we want to know how he reveals himself as a savior, then we have to have this book of words.

It's also necessary, not only for salvation, but for the proper worship of God, and also for how we are to live in response. Why is God's law written down? We have this from Psalm 78, which tells us that there is an aspect of remembrance, but there's also a warning. I'm in Psalm 78, starting in verse five, if you'd like to follow along. It says:

> 5 For He established a testimony in Jacob
> And set a law in Israel,
> Which He commanded our fathers
> That they should teach them to their children,
> 6 That the generation to come might know, even the children yet to be born,
> That they may arise and recount them to their children,
> 7 That they should set their confidence in God
> And not forget the deeds of God,
> But observe His commandments,
> 8 And not be like their fathers,
> A stubborn and rebellious generation,
> A generation that did not prepare its heart
> And whose spirit was not faithful to God.[13]

So God's word gives us a reminder. It gives us the basis for not wandering from what he has revealed to us. So here's where we see a repetition of God's covenant name, *Yahweh*. And that is the particular name that he used to reveal himself to Moses when he calls Moses to go to Pharaoh. And Moses says to God, *who should I tell him is sending me with this*

[13] Ps 78:5-8 (LSB).

message? And he reveals himself as *I am who I am*. And so that is the name by which he identifies himself with his special people.

In Psalm 19:7-9, there is a six-fold repetition regarding the law, both what it is and what it does. So we have words like *law*, *testimony*, *precepts*, *commandments*, and then *the fear of Yahweh*, *the judgments of Yahweh*. And a word that's probably familiar to you is the word *torah*, which refers first of all to the law. We might think of the commandments, but it also comes to be referring to the books of Moses, and in so doing, in generalizing that way, it really comes to refer to all of God's written revelation. We see that the law is *perfect*, it's *sure*, it's *right*, it's *pure*, it's *clean*, it's *true*. It's almost as if we're trying to think of as many different ways as we can to describe this law. And what it does, it *restores*, it makes *wise*, it brings us to *rejoicing*, it's *enlightening*, it's *enduring*. It's an effectual law, it doesn't just sit there. Again, Spurgeon says this:

> The gospel is perfect in all its parts and perfect as a whole. It is a crime to add to it, treason to alter it and felony to take from it.

All of it is necessary for life and faith.

While nature is a certain witness, scripture itself says that there's an even more certain witness, and that is the scripture. This is how Peter describes it, 2 Peter 1:19. He says:

> And we have as more sure the prophetic word, to which you do well to pay attention as to a lamp shining in a dark place, until the day dawns and the morning star arises in your hearts.[14]

And we see some of that same literary expression in Peter's epistle that we're seeing in the psalm itself. We're told in verse 10 that this law is *more desirable than gold* and *sweeter than honey*. And listen to how a few other portions of scripture describe it. Psalm 12, verse six:

> The words of Yahweh are pure words;
> As silver tried in a furnace on the ground, refined seven times.[15]

And the number seven there refers to removing all possible impurity from it.

In Psalm 119, verse 160, David says this:

---

[14] 2 Pet 1:19 (LSB).

[15] Ps 12:6 (LSB).

> The sum of Your word is truth,
> And every one of Your righteous judgments is everlasting.[16]

And then what is it worth? Again, David in Psalm 119, in verse 72:

> The law of Your mouth is better to me
> Than thousands of gold and silver pieces.[17]

How many is thousands? We could think of it like this, it's *all of it*, no matter how much you accumulate. We saw last time when we looked at Psalm 49, that wisdom cannot have a price tag put on it. It is worth more than all the gold and silver in the world.

We don't have to look very hard to find out what happens when men are without God's word. Here Solomon says in Proverbs 29:18:

> Where there is no vision, the people are out of control,
> But how blessed is he who keeps the law.[18]

And what do we see except a land that is out of control as we speak, having abandoned the word of God?

---

[16] Ps 119:160 (LSB).

[17] Ps 119:72 (LSB).

[18] Prov 29:18 (LSB).

The last portion of this psalm, the law exposes our sin. Now it's going to get a little personal. Verse 12:

> 12 Who can discern his errors? Acquit me of hidden faults.
> 13 Also keep back Your slave from presumptuous sins;
> Let them not rule over me;
> Then I will be blameless,
> And I shall be acquitted of great transgression.
> 14 Let the words of my mouth and the meditation of my heart
> Be acceptable in Your sight,
> O Yahweh, my rock and my Redeemer.

So the law is like the sun in the sense that it exposes everything it comes in contact with. Now, the problem that we have is that we have a sin problem in the heart and it takes the law of God to reveal that. I want you to see how the word of God is described like a surgical blade in the book of Hebrews chapter four, verse 12. We're told:

> For the word of God is living and active and sharper than any two-edged sword, and piercing as far as the division of soul and spirit, of both joints and marrow, and able to judge the thoughts and intentions of the heart.[19]

That ought to scare you a little bit.

Just how pervasive is sin? Again, we can go back to the psalms, Psalm 40:

---

[19] Heb 4:12 (LSB).

For evils beyond number have surrounded me;
My iniquities have overtaken me, so that I am not able to see;
They are more numerous than the hairs of my head,
And my heart has failed me.[20]

That's not very encouraging, but it gets worse—because it turns out that God sees all of that. This is from Psalm 90 verse eight. And this is a psalm that was written by Moses, interestingly enough, who went up on Mount Sinai to receive the law on the tablets of stone. He says:

You have set our iniquities before You,
Our secret sins in the light of Your presence.[21]

That law exposes every defect of the heart and the mind. So here's the great contrast that we have. The law shows us God's absolute perfection, but it also exposes man's absolute corruption. And it should drive us to a point of despair where we begin to ask, how do we get ourselves out of this? And the answer is that you can't do it, but God can. So the law gives us, I would say on the one hand, an antidote to prideful self-reliance. When we look at the law and understand how we have truly lived against the law, we understand that we can't rely on ourselves. But the law will be a faithful teacher to the one who takes heed of it. The law should be that thing which drives us to the Savior. And what is it that we're told at

---

[20] Ps 40:12 (LSB).

[21] Ps 90:8 (LSB).

the end of this psalm? We are driven back to the one who is called the Rock and the Redeemer. And what is the importance of the idea of one who is a *redeemer*? He is the one who *purchases* the one from slavery and brings him into his own ownership.

So here we come back to the idea of the master-slave relationship. And if it is upsetting to think of being a slave, let me put it this way, you're a slave one way or the other, because scripture says we are either *slaves to sin* or we are *slaves to righteousness*. So it's one or the other. Which is going to be our master, sin or Christ? That is the choice that scripture places before us. So it is that Redeemer who has, as we saw last time, the spiritual currency to purchase the soul from destruction. As we said last time, he is the one who goes into the grave and brings us out of the grave. He is the grave robber of God because he has gone into the grave by his own death and has come out by the power of an indestructible life.

As we begin to summarize, we could ask this question, and it's kind of a perplexing question. When we look at the universe, *why is it so big?* Did God need to make the universe as big as he did with as many stars and constellations as he did? And the answer is of course, *no*, he could have done something different. But here's what I want to consider. That perhaps he made the universe as big as he did so that when we look at the universe and cannot get our mind about the expanse of that universe and the power that's displayed in it, that we will say to ourselves, *the one who made it is bigger and more powerful than everything that we can see*. And again, that should bring glory back to God, the one who made it.

William Graham Scroggie summarizes it like this:

> In the skies is revealed his glory, in the scriptures, his greatness, and in the soul, his grace.

Luther also thought that this psalm was pointing to the gospel. He says, paraphrasing, *the psalm is a prophecy of the gospel as it was intended to go forth into all the world in all tongues*, so that every nation, tribe, people will hear the gospel and will be called by it.

Natural revelation is enough to know there is a God, but it's not enough to know his law and his salvation. God's power is not only revealed in the creation of the universe, but in the recreation of the fallen heart. And that's the good news. He can *purify* it, he can *preserve* it, and he can *perfect* it. And that is why we must turn to him.

In 1 John 1, we see that the light has come into the world. The sun runs its course, but there is another light that has come into the world. Listen to the words of John here:

> And this is the message we have heard from Him and declare to you, that God is Light, and in Him there is no darkness at all.
>
> If we say that we have fellowship with Him and yet walk in the darkness, we lie and do not do the truth; but if we walk in the Light as He Himself is in the Light, we have fellowship with one another, and the blood of Jesus His Son cleanses us from all sin. If we say that we have no sin, we deceive ourselves and the truth is not in us. If we confess our sins, He is faithful and righteous to forgive us our sins and to cleanse us from all unrighteousness. If we say that we have not sinned, we make Him a liar and His word is not in us.[22]

That is the call of the gospel. And if you have not yet stepped into the light of the glory of God in Jesus Christ for salvation, for rescue from sin, I urge you to do that today.

Jesus himself says in response:

> "Let your light shine before men in such a way that they may see your good works, and glorify your Father who is in heaven."[23]

Amen.

---

[22] 1 John 1:5-10 (LSB).

[23] Matt 5:16 (LSB).

Father, we thank you for this word that you've given us today, and I pray that it will be an encouragement to everyone who hears, and that those who do not yet know you savingly will flee to you for salvation when they see in the law the sin of their own heart. Turn the rest of us from our sins. Help us to walk in righteousness, holy lives before you, and in Christ's name we pray. Amen.

God's Building Plan (Psalm 127)

January 8, 2023

Today our message comes from the 127th psalm, a short psalm of five verses. And I'll be reading and teaching today from what's called the *Legacy Standard* version of this psalm. Let me read the psalm and please give your attention to it.

1 Unless Yahweh builds the house,
They labor in vain who build it;
Unless Yahweh watches the city,
The watchman keeps awake in vain.
2 It is in vain that you rise up early,
That you sit out late,
O you who eat the bread of painful labors;
For in this manner, He gives sleep to His beloved.

3 Behold, children are an inheritance of Yahweh,
The fruit of the womb is a reward.
4 Like arrows in the hand of a warrior,
So are the children of one's youth.
5 How blessed is the man who fills his quiver with them;
They will not be ashamed
When they speak with enemies in the gate.[24]

This is the reading of God's word today.

---

[24] Ps 127 (LSB). Quoted again afterward.

The title of our message is *God's Building Plan*. And what we see right away is the prominence of God as the builder who's described in this psalm. This is subtitled *a Psalm of Solomon*. There's some question about whether it was Solomon who wrote it or if it was perhaps David, his father, who wrote it for him. In either case, it dates from that time period between the kingship of David and Solomon. And we notice that this is also similar to one of the psalms we looked at a few weeks ago, Psalm 49, which is what we call a *wisdom* psalm. This one is also a wisdom psalm, meaning that it's not specifically a prayer. So that should attract our interest—that there is something of knowledge or wisdom that this psalm seeks to teach us. And it's also called the *Builder's Psalm*, an appropriate title. So I'll start by looking at the first two verses.

This psalm divides up naturally into the first two verses and then the last three. The first part we'll call *the futility of self-reliance*. The futility of self-reliance.

Let me read those verses again.

> 1 Unless Yahweh builds the house,
> They labor in vain who build it;
> Unless Yahweh watches the city,
> The watchman keeps awake in vain.
> 2 It is in vain that you rise up early,
> That you sit out late,

> O you who eat the bread of painful labors;
> For in this manner, He gives sleep to His beloved.

From the very opening verse, we see that—if we could put it this way—that Yahweh—God—is the central character of the psalm. And notice the name, *Yahweh*. Now, if you're from Baptist circles, you might be accustomed to referring to God in his covenant name as *Jehovah*. That's another way that his covenant name has been translated. The *Legacy Standard Bible* renders it *Yahweh*, which in most English translations is *the* LORD with the little capital letters. That's actually the covenant name of God. And it's an important way that he identifies himself as the God of his special people. So it has rich meaning when we see that name of God, Yahweh, appear like this, especially when it's repeated.

Now interestingly, we notice that this is stated as though everything depends upon him. Notice it says twice, *unless Yahweh . . . unless Yahweh*. And it indicates to us that no matter what else happens, *unless Yahweh*, nothing much matters or nothing much counts. But doesn't human effort count for something? And again, the answer comes from this psalm, *unless Yahweh*. Otherwise, we have the other refrain, that all of the effort that we expend is *in vain*. And it's repeated three times, *in vain . . . in vain . . . in vain*. What does that mean? What does the scripture mean when it talks about *in vain* or *vanity*? It means *futility*, that you're working, but in the end, you're really not accomplishing much.

Let's now think about who else is mentioned in this psalm. We notice at the end of verse two, that it refers to *his Beloved . . . his Beloved . . . the Beloved of Yahweh*, whose labor is in him. And it also mentions toward the end of the psalm, those apart from God who are named as *enemies*. So we have Yahweh, we have all work being done to him and through him, and we have those who are doing that referred to as *his beloved*, and those who are apart from him referred to as *his enemies*. It's very stark language—a very stark contrast as we often find in the psalms.

There's another character that we want to mention as well. And that's the character that shows up in the second part of the psalm. And who is that? It's *children*, the children of the one who trusts in God. Now we notice, of course, that this is poetry. And so there's a poetic play on words here when it says that *man* and *Yahweh* either *build* or *watch*. It doesn't mean in the same sense, obviously. So a little bit of a word play with that idea of *building* or *watching*. But we also realize that at least in one sense, it is Yahweh who is behind it all—because it is Yahweh who makes man and gives him the work to do and the strength to do it.

An important idea in this psalm is the idea of God's *providence*—that God is controlling all things. And he's bringing about the ends that he has designed for the work that we do. And our task is to be in alignment with the work that he would have us to do so that it brings about his desired ends. So God controls both the *work* and the *results* of the work.

God is in every sphere of life as well. We see these mentioned. We can talk about the sphere of the *home*, and the *workplace*—where one does his labor in the *fields*, for example. We could also mention labor that's done in the *church* and for the church, and labor that's carried out in *society*. All of these are spheres where work is being done. Man is doing the work. And then the important question is whether Yahweh is in the work or whether man is attempting to do it out of his own effort. We get this conclusion that it is God who ultimately either establishes the work or demolishes it. And God can demolish any works of man that are contrary to what he desires.

So, no man can build apart from the God who makes him. No man can build in a way that ever thwarts God's plans. And that's good news, especially in troubling times—that God's plans can never be undone by man's efforts. No man's work can fail either when God is working *for* him and working *through* him. If man cannot build the very least thing without God's assistance, then he can by no means build the greater things. In other words, if a man cannot build his own home without God, then he can't build a neighborhood or a village, a town, a city, a society, a nation. All of these things must be done *in* and *through* God or else the house begins to crumble.

Now, it is the case that man can—and often does—work in a way that opposes God's purposes. And the man who sets himself in opposition to God is also inviting God's judgment against him. How do we work against him? The simplest explanation—or the simplest answer—is that when we work against his *law*. He has revealed what he desires in our behavior, in our choices and in the law. And when we work against that, we are most certainly building a work that will crumble. We notice as well, there's nothing wrong with the idea of work. God works. We read in the very opening verses of Genesis that God has worked to bring about his creation, that he worked for six days and finished the work and declared that it was very good. And then he did what at the end of it? He rested on that seventh day. So in the work that we do, we're imitating the pattern of God himself in his work and in his rest.

What is the difference between the builders in this psalm? We see first of all a man who relies on his own strength. And the man who relies on his own strength is building for his own benefit and probably for his own credit. As we saw in one of our earlier psalms, it's very tempting for a man who wants to make a name for himself to name things after himself—something that will last after he is gone. He's building to gain his own credit. Now it's interesting that there's a contrast in this psalm, not between the one who *works* and the one who *doesn't* work, but between the two who work, one according to the *Lord* and one on his *own* effort. In other words, this psalm doesn't tell us anything about idlers or sluggards as the Proverbs call it—those who just refuse to work. These are people who are working hard, but what they're doing is they're working hard in their own effort and finding that their work is ultimately unsatisfactory. The man who relies on God's strength will be building for God's glory and not for his own. So there's the contrast between those who build by Yahweh's strength—and with his purposes—and those who try to do it without him.

What is the manner of man's work? Does any of man's work stand forever? And all we have to do is look at the ruins all over the world—from ancient history all the way to the present day—of man's works that have failed and will fail. As hard as it might be to acknowledge it, much of what we see around us today that we think is so spectacular in terms of achievement will one day come to ruins. And that simply illustrates the principle—that work done without God's strength and without his intervention is work that will ultimately crumble. On the other hand, any labor that's expended for God is part of what helps us build treasures in heaven. Scripture tells us about that, doesn't it? *Do not store up for yourselves treasures on earth where moth and rust destroy, but build treasure for yourself in heaven where moth and rust do not destroy*. And I don't want to forget the other part too, *where thieves do not break in and steal*. There's a place where we can build our treasure, even begin to build it now, where that treasure will last forever. So all the cities of man, even those that are built with God's favor, will eventually pass into nothingness. At the end of the age, everything in this life comes to an end, but we're told that there is a *building*, there is a *city* that is designed and built by God that is an eternal city. And Abraham is commended in the book of Hebrews for looking forward to the city that would be designed and built by God. It will be a dwelling place for his people forever.

What is it that makes man's work futile? It's done for selfish purposes. And in the end, it has no lasting value. It may build some worldly fame or some worldly wealth, but it doesn't last. That first song that we sang today was a great selection providentially—warning us about building things on earth and not looking for a treasure in heaven. Such work will be burned up in the fire of judgment and that work will all perish. And the tragic part of that is not so much that the work will perish, but the worker who has not placed his reliance on Yahweh will also perish with his work.

Even the man of God—the pastor, the preacher, the teacher—has to give care to his work or else he could suffer loss. Paul warns about that in his first letter to the Corinthians, that *every man's work will be tested by fire and anything that is wood, hay or stubble is going to be burned up*. And that the man may survive the test himself, but there may not be much left of his work if he did not build well.

In another part of 1 Corinthians—when Paul is addressing the divisions in the Corinthian church—he reminds the Corinthians that there's one who plants, and he's referring to himself there, one who waters, where he's referring to Apollos, and then he says this, that *it is God who gives the growth*. In other words, Paul doesn't deserve credit for starting the Corinthian church and Apollos doesn't deserve credit for moving it along, but it's God who is working through those men to bring about his desired ends. It is the Spirit who gives life to the work and makes it fruitful. And if the Spirit is not in the work, then it falls to the ground.

Why do we fall into this trap of false confidence and self-reliance? The satisfaction of our work should come from doing our work unto the Lord. And here we may have to work by faith rather than by sight, meaning that the work that we do may not produce immediate results. It may not produce the kind of spectacular results that we would like to see, that we can glory in. But working by faith, as Paul did in Corinth, he started that congregation and years later it was continuing under the work of other men. So we start our work by faith and it's God who makes it fruitful.

And we remember that our relationship to God is that we are servants of him and that it is our task to be faithful servants in order to please our master.

How does trouble and hardship help to break our self-reliance if we're falling into this temptation? Well, for one thing, it shows us that nothing made by human hands can endure forever. Sometimes we do see our work crumble to the ground. What we have worked so hard for and stored up may disappear in a moment, just as it did in the case of Job when he was tested. But when we have lost our worldly possessions, we reach that point—rock bottom as we say—where there's no place to turn except to God. So bringing us back into reliance on God may be one of the effects of having loss in the things we have labored for.

The psalmist in his wisdom is telling us that the one who toils in his own effort finds little refreshment from his rest. He takes his rest, but it's not satisfying rest. His labor is never enough to satisfy his deepest needs because he's doing it for himself rather than for God. Meanwhile, we see that the one who toils for the Lord rests securely. He not only rests because he's tired, but he rests because his confidence is in God to guard the work that he's done and to multiply it even while he sleeps. We have verses like this that tell us that *the farmer sleeps not knowing how his crop grows, that his crop continues to grow even while he takes his rest*. And then we have this assurance from Psalm 121, that *he who keeps Israel, Yahweh, neither slumbers nor sleeps*. God never dozes off. He is always overseeing his work.

Rest itself should be seen as a gift from God. And here we can think in three terms. The psalm chiefly points to the *daily* rest that we take—daily rest refreshes us for our daily labor. We are told, as it were, *to work while it is day*. Meanwhile, we also have a *weekly* rest. What do we call this day that we take weekly rest, to take time to be in the congregation, to worship? We call it the *Sabbath*, and that simply means *rest*. And so from the very beginning, when God completed his work and took his rest, he established the pattern for us of six days of work and a day of rest, where we turn our hearts and our minds to him. And then there's a rest yet to come, isn't there? There is an *eternal* rest that delivers us from all the toil and the care of this life and into the rewards of eternity. And that is where the saints will rest from all their labors. So work and rest is to be done unto the Lord. And in that we find our profit.

The rest of this psalm gets a little more specific. I'll call this next part, *the blessing of a home built by God*. Let me read the last three verses.

> 3 Behold, children are an inheritance of Yahweh,
> The fruit of the womb is a reward.

4 Like arrows in the hand of a warrior,
So are the children of one's youth.
5 How blessed is the man who fills his quiver with them;
They will not be ashamed
When they speak with enemies in the gate.

There is a sudden change in the tone of this psalm at this point. And some have suggested that maybe the first part of the psalm doesn't belong with the second part. But if we look at it a little more closely, it seems as though that second part of the psalm actually fits very nicely with the first part. What is the purpose after all of *building*, whether it's a home or whether it's a town, a city, a nation, if we're not building it for *people*? And where are the people going to come from? They're going to come from our *posterity*. So we see the connection between the physical labor of building houses, of farming and harvesting and that sort of thing, and the home where there's a different kind of labor that takes place, and that is the labor of bringing forth children and raising up children.

When the psalmist talks about children being an inheritance, the proper understanding of this is not that they are the inheritance of their *parents*, but that they're an inheritance of *Yahweh*, who is the one who gives them. And if that's so, then the parents are merely stewards of what God has given them for a time. Do we know that our children belong to him? And do we raise them in such a way that we always remember that they are ultimately his to give, and even to take, as he sees fit?

We notice that children are called *the fruit of the womb*. So as a man labors in the field to produce *bread*, so the woman labors in the home to raise *children*. And maybe it's not very politically correct to say this, but in fact, it is true that there is a difference between men and women. And there's a difference between the callings of men and women from the very beginning, as God designed the family. Now, unfortunately in our own society, we selfishly are prone to see our children not as a blessing, but as an obstacle, a hindrance. And that's a significant change from the recent past. And when we think about the decline of culture and where things are going, we're going to look back someday and realize that we destroyed society because we turned against our own children.

There's always a concern: if we have children, will we have enough to eat? Will we have a place to live and so forth? But the one who trusts in the Lord can say that *when God sends mouths, he will also send bread*. Because remember what we just said—that the children are *his* inheritance. Children are the most precious possession, even when we have little in the way of material wealth. And there was a 17th century teacher who said this, that *children are the possessions that make the poor man rich*. Where do we see our riches? Do we see it in our *possessions* or do we see it in our *families*? And that's the question: do we see children as a *blessing* or a *curse*? And unfortunately, too many today see children as a curse—a thing to be avoided.

Scripture calls that man blessed, not only who has *children*, but also lives long enough to see his *grandchildren*. I'm willing to bet some of you have lived long enough to see your own grandchildren and to find encouragement in what you see, knowing that your own work many years ago was certainly not in vain as you raised your own children. But meanwhile, our society considers it a blessing to have no children at all. We are raising it to a new kind of value that we have childless couples these days. Maybe they have pets, but children are too much work and too much of a cost. And that's tragic. We have forgotten that God's promises are not only for us, but also for our children. They're to be passed from generation to generation. And this is part of the significance of what it means for God to be a *covenant* God with his people. That is not merely those to whom he makes the promise, but that the promise passes from generation to generation as he continues to build his church.

In that first stanza, we saw that there are two kinds of men and two results, blessing for the one who labors in the Lord and futility or frustration for the one who labors for himself. In other words, we're either going to work under the yoke of God for his glory, or we're going to become his enemy. Those are the only two possibilities. God makes it clear in his word that there are only two kinds of man—those who are saved and those who are lost. And those who are lost—who have put themselves against him—have become his enemy. And if that's the case, then God's enemies also become the enemies of his people—*his beloved*—as we saw in those first verses. And in that case, conflict is inevitable. So we have this word picture at the end of the psalm about children being *arrows in the quiver*. The warrior has arrows in his quiver to fight, as it were, the spiritual battle. And that even there's this warning that the enemies are at the gates of the city. And who is going to defend the city? Who is going to defend the home against the enemies of God? Children become a defensive weapon in that battle. Our enemies are at the gates, at the doorstep, so to speak, but the children become our defense in that day of trouble. And if we see children in this way, that they are arrows of the warrior in the spiritual battle, then we should think it's a small sacrifice that we invest in their care, because we may soon need them to defend the house.

As we begin to close, I want to leave you with a few exhortations, a few things for you to use to apply what we're learning today. The first is to give yourself to the work, that it's still the case that effort counts for something. And the scripture says it this way, *whatever your hand finds to do, do it with all your might*. Don't fall into the futility or the despair of thinking that your work doesn't count so there's no reason to put any effort into it.

And to remember—and I think part of the lesson from this psalm is that there is no labor that is menial when it's done to the Lord. We too often tend to think in terms of jobs as being more important or less important. And yet scripture tells us that everything that we do to the Lord receives a reward.

Another important lesson is that we should not fret. Scripture repeatedly warns us against fretfulness, against anxiety, against the uncertainty of what's going to happen. So do not fall into the trap of fretfulness. Remember that God is in control of all things.

Trust God to make your work fruitful. He is the one who can make a faithful effort produce a one hundred fold harvest. It's a remarkable thing. And perhaps because we don't do much farming these days, the idea is that we could plant a crop expecting to get a harvest equivalent to the crop. Then scripture says that God can take a regular effort that would produce a regular crop and multiply it by a hundred. That is the difference for those who rely on God for the product of their work.

And lastly, if you do not yet trust in Christ for salvation, you have to start there. Put yourself under the blessing of Yahweh. He stands ready to receive you into his family and you will become part of that temple of living stones that he is building up with Christ as the chief cornerstone.

That is the house that will last forever. That is the city that Abraham was looking forward to. So *unless Yahweh builds the house, they who build, build in vain*. Let all that you do be done in dependence upon his strength. Let your work be done to his glory, and you will be storing up your treasure in heaven. Count your daily rest as a blessing, and know that the greater blessing of eternal rest still awaits for those who put their trust in him.

Amen.

Let's pray. Thank you, Father, for this word. I pray that you would apply it to each of our hearts. Make us ready and able to hear what you have said to us today. Through your word, let us put our confidence in you for all the work that we do, whatever it may be, whether small or large. And I pray your blessing upon these people today. In Christ's name. Amen.

Near to the Brokenhearted (Psalm 34)

March 26, 2023

Today we're going to be looking at Psalm 34 from the *Legacy Standard Bible* (LSB). We have a few copies of that you can share as we look at that. I'm going to do something a little differently today. Rather than starting with the reading of the psalm, I'm going to start with the background. Because this particular psalm actually has a very interesting background. And for us to have a better sense of what David is praying about and what he's praising God for, it's helpful for us to know a little bit about the story.

The subtitle on this psalm gives us an important clue. First of all, it tells us that it is *a Psalm of David*. And then it says that *when he feigned madness before Abimelech, so that he drove him away and he departed*. Now, what is that referring to? Well, that's what the backstory is going to be about before we get to the reading of the psalm.

First a little background. We see that it's attributed to David, that there was a particular occasion where he was literally running for his life because Saul, the first of the kings of Israel, had become jealous and angry and was determined to find David and kill him. He did not want David as a competitor. This psalm is not a prayer *per se*. But we'll see that's very interesting because God is mentioned throughout this psalm according to his personal name, *Yahweh*. So we can think of this as a commemorative event, a commemorative psalm. David is giving us a recollection of something that had happened at a particular time of distress and a response, as well as an exhortation. The response that we see from David in this psalm is the response of *worship*. And the exhortation that he's going to have for all the rest of us is to *fear God*. And he's going to give us some very important instructions about what it means to fear God.

You'll notice on the handout that this is what's called an *acrostic psalm*, meaning that it's written according to a pattern that the beginning of each verse follows the letters of the Hebrew alphabet. And there are several psalms that are written in this particular fashion. The 119th Psalm is the one that is the most well known of those. But this is also an acrostic psalm, and that gives us a clue that it was meant to be memorized and to be known.

Spurgeon describes this psalm as

> A combination of a hymn, the first half, and a sermon in the second half.

So we'll be looking at it in that context. And this is a very personal psalm, as we'll see, where David is in a terrible strife at this particular moment and is looking to God for his deliverance.

Now the circumstances. How did we get here? To get the history we have to go to the book of 1 Samuel, and there are actually five, and a little bit of six chapters, that give us the backstory that tell us why David wrote this psalm. Don't worry, I'm not going to read those five or six chapters. I'm going to do my best in the next few minutes to give you a summary of what's going on, in part because, in typical fashion, there is some very interesting irony that's taking place here behind the scenes.

We're familiar with the story of Goliath, the giant. And Goliath was from a Philistine town called Gath. That's going to be a very important detail a little later on in the story. So Goliath comes out to face the Israelite army. For forty days, morning and evening, he goes out to the armies of Israel and taunts them and says, *send out one of your brave champions to fight me. And whichever of us wins, those will serve the other*. Well, while this was going on, David was actually back at home helping keep his father's sheep. Three of his older brothers were serving in the army, so they were on the front lines of the battle. But David's father, Jesse, sent David on an errand to take provisions to the army, to his brothers, and to some of the officers, and then to bring back a report to find out what was going on. So David goes to the front lines, and as he does that, he hears Goliath now coming out again to taunt the armies of Israel. And because no one else in the Israelite army was willing to go out and face this guy, David said, *I'll do it.* And there was a bit of mockery about that because David was a shepherd, he wasn't a soldier. And what was David's answer? He says, *whenever the lion or the bear attacked the flock, I set upon the lion and the bear and killed him. And I'll do the same thing to this guy*. He was a remarkably brave young man. So he goes out and fights Goliath. We know how that story turned out. He strikes Goliath in the forehead with a stone. Goliath falls flat on his face. David comes up to him, takes Goliath's sword—which is going to be another important detail—and uses that sword of Goliath to cut off Goliath's head. Consequently, the Israelite army is emboldened, the Philistine army is terrified, they run, the Israelites chase after them, and Israel wins a great victory that day because of David's bravery.

What happened immediately after that? Well, a number of the women were singing a victory song. And that was the source of the friction between David and Saul because the victory song was, *Saul has slain his thousands and David has slain his ten thousands*. And Saul didn't like that. It made him very angry. So it started what was going to be a long conflict between Saul and David until Saul was finally killed in a battle with the Philistines.

Saul determines that he's going to kill David. The first thing he tries to do is throwing a spear at him, trying to pin him to the wall. David dodges the spear and avoids being killed on that occasion. Now, one of the interesting things about Saul in his madness is how graphically the Bible describes Saul's mental illness. By modern standards, we would say that Saul is a paranoid schizophrenic. He's paranoid that David is going to try to take the throne away from him, but he's also a schizophrenic in terms of how quickly he goes from saying, *David, my son, I would never hurt a hair on your head*, to trying to kill him again. Very interesting. We might even suggest that the scripture is indicating that Saul was somehow possessed by a demon and overthrown at times.

We see an echo here of Cain and Abel. We remember the sacrifices that Cain and Abel made. And God accepted Abel's sacrifice and he rejected Cain's sacrifice and consequently Cain hated his brother Abel and was determined to kill him. And the parallel here is that it wasn't that Cain was angry at his brother *per se*. Who was he really angry with? He was angry at God. Abel was just a convenient proxy.

Now Saul tries by a number of different ways to get David killed. One of the ways that he does this is to promise his daughter Michal to David as a wife if David will go and kill 200 Philistines. And really what Saul had in mind was for the Philistines to kill David. But David was victorious, brought back the proof that he had killed the Philistines, and was given Michal as a wife. Not long after that, Michal would help him escape from Saul's plot to kill him. So over and over again, Saul is persecuting and trying to kill David. Every time the Philistines engaged Israel in battle, David goes out, and among those who are fighting for the Israelite army, he's the most successful. So over and over again—this is an important theme—David is victorious over the Philistines.

The next thing that Saul tries to do is to get his servants to kill David. And that included Jonathan, his son. And Jonathan was loyal to David. So Jonathan warned David that his father was trying to kill him. Saul then, at the urging of Jonathan in one of his saner moments, relents of his intent to kill David. Then there's another war with the Philistines. David wins another decisive victory. We might say (in the modern language) that David *owned* the Philistines. Anytime he went out to battle with the Philistines, God gave him victory over them. Again, Saul tries to kill David with a spear over and over again. At that point, David escaped and fled to Samuel, the priest. Saul pursued him, but his plans were thwarted by the Holy Spirit in a rather ironic way. So David returns to Jonathan and Jonathan tries to assure him that he is safe from Saul. In response, David suggested a test. *Let's find out. I'll be absent from the king's table and we'll see how the king reacts*. So Jonathan goes along with this plan. Saul becomes enraged at Jonathan when he realizes that Jonathan was covering for David, and even tries to kill his own son at that point, at which point Jonathan understands that his father is determined to kill David. So he ends up making a pact with David.

David flees for his life, literally, with virtually nothing but the shirt on his back. He doesn't have any provisions. He doesn't even have a weapon, and he has nobody else with him. He's literally by himself at this point. Where does he go? And here's where part of the irony is. But first he flees to Ahimelech the priest, where he receives a provision of bread and a sword. And guess what sword it was that he received? It was the sword of Goliath that he received on that occasion. From there he flees to Achish, to the king of Gath. Now who was from Gath? Goliath was from Gath. David has a sword. Whose sword does he have? He's got Goliath's sword. And by the way, the Philistines haven't forgotten the song that the women sang when David was victorious over Goliath. So upon the reminder that the Philistines have every reason to be angry with him, David fakes insanity. And by virtue of faking insanity, Achish says, *why do I want a madman in my midst? Get him out of here*. And from there he flees. That is the occasion for which this psalm has been written. So that is the backstory. And if you want to spend some time looking at that more, you might read those chapters starting in 1 Samuel 17 this afternoon.

So with that, now let me turn to the text of the psalm and read through this text. Have in mind all that's just happened to David as we come to this psalm.[25]

He says:

1 I will bless Yahweh at all times;
His praise shall continually be in my mouth.

2 My soul will make its boast in Yahweh;
The humble will hear it and rejoice.

3 O magnify Yahweh with me,
And let us exalt His name together.

4 I inquired of Yahweh, and He answered me,
And delivered me from all that I dread.

5 They looked to Him and were radiant,
And their faces will never be humiliated.

6 This poor man called out, and Yahweh heard him
And saved him out of all his troubles.

7 The angel of Yahweh encamps around those who fear Him,
And rescues them.

8 O taste and see that Yahweh is good;
How blessed is the man who takes refuge in Him!

---

[25] The acrostic divisions have been omitted from the text.

9 Oh, fear Yahweh, you His saints;
For there is no want to those who fear Him.

10 The young lions do lack and suffer hunger;
But they who inquire of Yahweh shall not be in want of any good thing.

11 Come, you children, listen to me;
I will teach you the fear of Yahweh.

12 Who is the man who delights in life
And loves many days that he may see good?

13 Guard your tongue from evil
And your lips from speaking deceit.

14 Depart from evil and do good;
Seek peace and pursue it.

15 The eyes of Yahweh are toward the righteous
And His ears are open to their cry for help.

16 The face of Yahweh is against evildoers,
To cut off the memory of them from the earth.

17 The righteous cry, and Yahweh hears
And delivers them out of all their troubles.

18 Yahweh is near to the brokenhearted
And saves those who are crushed in spirit.

19 Many are the evils against the righteous,
But Yahweh delivers him out of them all.

20 He keeps all his bones,
Not one of them is broken.

21 Evil shall slay the wicked,
And those who hate the righteous will be condemned.

22 Yahweh redeems the soul of His slaves,
And all those who take refuge in Him will not be condemned.[26]

That's the Word of God.

As we begin to look at this psalm, something that stands out very clearly to us from the first are the contrasts. Fairly typical of Hebrew poetry that we have this contrast. And what is the specific contrast? It's between the *righteous* and the *wicked*. So we see two kinds of people who are presented here, and only those two. They're named in various ways and we'll look at some of those. Who are the righteous? They are the ones who fear Yahweh. They are also called slaves or saints of Yahweh. The wicked are those who do not fear God. But we also notice that the wicked are the ones who are persecuting the righteous. So there's a contrast, but there's also a *conflict* that goes along with that contrast. And again, what's in behind all of this is the conflict between David who's fleeing from Saul and Saul who's trying to kill him. So we find David as that *saint* who is in turmoil because of his enemies, and it is God he is seeking for deliverance.

[26] Ps 34 (LSB). Quoted again afterward.

And here's another contrast then, that the righteous are those who seek God in their affliction, while the wicked are those who are opposed to God and turn their backs on him.

Something that's noteworthy about this psalm, and it is evident in this translation called the *Legacy Standard Bible*, and that is throughout this psalm we see the personal covenant name of God being used. It's the name that he used to reveal himself to Moses. And just as Moses spoke to God in a face-to-face manner—and you'll remember that caused Moses' face to shine—so David also reflects the radiance of his personal communion with God, which he says, *whose face will never be ashamed.*

Now there's an ultimate contrast between the righteous and the wicked. And it is that the wicked are *condemned* and the righteous are *redeemed.* And not just in the body, but also in the spirit. We must add that, when we talk about those who are righteous, we're not talking about those who are *self-righteous*. That's actually a sign of hypocrisy. So this psalm contains a word of assurance for those who are among the righteous, but it's also a word of warning for those who are counted among the wicked. The righteous will be vindicated and delivered from their enemies. The wicked will be judged and condemned.

In the New Testament, we have this idea of a broad road and a narrow road. The broad road that leads to *destruction*, whereupon many travel. The narrow road that leads to *life*, which is found by few. And the world gets those mixed up very easily. So we have many who are on the broad road who think they are on the narrow road.

How is it that we're going to become numbered among those who are righteous? David gives us some important points here. We'll see that the psalm contains an instructional interlude. Suddenly the voice of the psalm changes and says, *come children and listen to me. Come and be instructed*. What is the subject? The fear of Yahweh. We understand that to mean the *salvation* that comes from the fear of Yahweh. What does that accomplish? That gives us the blessings of God, and particularly long life. That's what he questions us with. *Who wants long life?* And not just long life in this life, but in fact, eternal life. Who wants salvation? Well, in some sense, everyone wants salvation, but there's a certain way to obtain it, as David is going to give to us. Who are the ones who are ready to receive salvation? David gives us important clues. The one who is brokenhearted. The one who is crushed in spirit. The one who can honestly call himself poor. And think of David in this condition. He is running for his life. He has virtually nothing but the shirt on his back. He's by himself. He's describing himself as poor. He recognizes his weakness. He recognizes his sin. He is fearful. He is grieved. He is alone.

He is desperate. He is hungry. What will salvation produce? Salvation will produce gratitude and will turn to praise. So that's how we can begin to recognize when salvation comes.

How is that salvation to be obtained? By walking in God's commandments. David lists these things, *speaking truth and not deception*, *departing from evil*, *doing good*, *seeking peace*, and *pursuing it*, which is to say, not being engaged in creating strife, conflict, and so forth. We could say that this list of do's and don'ts summarizes the second Great Commandment, *to love your neighbor as yourself, because love does no harm to a neighbor*. And that duty of man towards man comes with a promise. You remember the Fifth Commandment, *Honor your father and mother that you may live long in the land that the LORD your God is giving you.*

Having said that, we have to remember that there is no promise of universal salvation. God is love, but only towards those who fear him and trust him and follow him. Everyone else remains under the fearful expectation of judgment—that broad road I mentioned which leads to destruction for everyone on it who thinks that he can make his own road to eternal life. And that is the danger—that we create a religion out of our own imagination and think that we are in God's favor when we are not.

Obedience is the act of faith that connects us to the promises of God. We show our trust in God by doing his will, as he tells us. And interestingly, at this point we are told to *taste* God, that is, to prove that God will do what he promises to do for us. And obedience we can also understand as a form of repentance. If we are doing God's will, then that means we're *not* doing our own will. We are *forsaking* evil and *doing* good. And we are reminded that good works don't save us. Good works demonstrate that we have a new life, and we have new life in Christ. What is the posture of the true saint? He is humble, he is reverent, he is brokenhearted, crushed, submissive, dependent, not relying on anything in himself. Because as soon as we start relying on ourselves, we are departing from the grace of God.

The wicked man, by contrast, certainly wants the blessings. The problem is that the wicked man is willing to get those blessings any way that he can. Rather than through obedience, he's willing to take those things by force, by lying, by stealing, by oppressing the righteous, even murdering, stirring up strife and dissension and division, whatever it takes. The good news through this is that God's enemies, the wicked, can become his friends through the message of the gospel. Those who hate truth can love righteousness. Those who took Satan's side in the Fall can be reconciled to God. And in that, there is no better news in the universe.

Let's consider for a moment the blessings of righteousness and the destruction of the wicked. Now we know—and I'm preaching to the choir—that not all the promises of God are fun because he does not promise all the comforts that we might like to have in this life. In this world, every one of us is touched both by sin, and eventually, death. And there's a contrast between the afflictions of the body, which include things like persecution or privation or illness, and the afflictions of the soul and the spirit, such as anguish and guilt and disappointment. The question we face is when we have affliction, whether that affliction is a foretaste of future judgment—if we're numbered among the wicked—or whether that affliction is the pain that will drive us closer to God. For the righteous, all afflictions are temporary, and they are ultimately used for one's good. We have that promise throughout scripture. Meanwhile, for the wicked, afflictions serve as a warning of greater judgment yet to come. If it's the case that relief or deliverance, as David says, if it's only temporal, then it can't be very much comfort, especially for those who are afflicted in soul and spirit. Even when our body's needs are satisfied, we may still suffer a great pain of anguish, great affliction. We have to be careful that we don't confuse the spiritual blessings and the material blessings. We may have abundant material blessings, but that doesn't necessarily put us in the favor of God. And it's often when we lose our material blessings, God uses that for our chastisement and to bring us closer to him. The righteous are able to find spiritual blessings even in a time of hardship. The righteous are able to understand that God is using those things to draw him closer. Material blessings that are acquired by evil means are going to become a curse for the wicked that lasts for eternity. They may have something for a short time, but they will soon lose that and everything else.

This psalm tells us that God is going to *redeem his slaves*. Meaning what? He is going to bring them out of their slavery to sin and into slavery to him as righteous. And the greatest assurance that we have is that when God *purchases* a people for himself, he's going to protect his investment. It will not be lost. Not one will be lost.

It's striking in this psalm to see the nearness of God. How close is God? And the psalm speaks in this kind of language, that he is near enough for us to *taste*, he is near enough to *see*, he is near enough to *hear*, and he is near enough to *help*. There is no sense in this psalm that David is either being ignored or overlooked. God sees and hears and acts immediately and decisively when David cries out to him. David does not have to beg just to get an audience. He doesn't have to wait to get a response. In this case, God has heard and answered immediately in the midst of his present distress. And we notice as we think in terms of the fear of Yahweh, that the more we fear Yahweh, the less we fear man. We're told that Yahweh encamps between the wicked and the righteous. He becomes *deliverance* for the righteous and *destruction* for the wicked. We think of how God in his presence in the cloud stood between Israel and Egypt in the wilderness, so that it was *protection* for Israel and *judgment* for Egypt. He brought Israel through the waters of the Red Sea and called it baptism. And when the Egyptians tried to cross the Red Sea, the waters came upon them and drowned them. This is how God protects his people.

Having received salvation, what is our response? And the simple answer is *worship*, just as this psalm started. So we see in this psalm, in the praise that it raises for God, is that there's this connection to the first Great Commandment, for us to *love God with our heart, our soul, our mind, and our strength*. In the opening verses, we see that David is praising Yahweh at all times, meaning what? Whether in comfort or in hardship. We see that he makes his boast in Yahweh, and that others join in the praise with him. And then he urges others to join with him in worship.

Job is a stark reminder of suffering. And it's also a reminder that not all suffering is a result of sin, that suffering may often simply be a testing, a kind of testing. Our response in the midst of suffering is to praise God and have thankfulness even at those times. We remember that what we need, he provides for us, and that whatever would hinder us, he removes from us. And that in his giving and his taking, he reveals our true needs. What happens *to* us will reveal what is *in* us. It will expose our worthless idols of comfort and self-reliance. Only God can meet our deepest spiritual needs, and only he can defeat the last enemy so that we can have victory over the grave.

This psalm wraps back around on itself. We could very easily take those first three verses of praise and bring them down to the end as a response of praise. It goes like this:

1 I will bless Yahweh at all times;
His praise shall continually be in my mouth.

2 My soul will make its boast in Yahweh;
The humble will hear it and rejoice.

3 O magnify Yahweh with me,
And let us exalt His name together.

And that's a fitting way for us to be reminded that in all things, we are to worship God with our whole heart, mind, soul, and strength.

Let's pray. Father, we thank you for your word. We thank you that your word gives us a glimpse into the life of the saints like David, and it gives us a glimpse into the very heart of God. We pray that you would be with each and every one of us, strengthen us in our weakness, our illness, strengthen us as we face the days ahead. Help us to fully trust in you for all that we need, both in this life and the life to come. We pray in Christ's name. Amen.

The Futility of Rebellion (Psalm 2)

May 21, 2023

Today we're going to give our attention to Psalm 2. If you can find your Psalter in the Bible, then it's probably on the first page. I'm going to be reading from a translation called the *Legacy Standard Bible*, which as I've mentioned in the past, I like this translation because it renders the name of God as *Yahweh* and not *the LORD*. So you'll notice that as we read through it. It's a fairly short psalm, twelve verses. It fits nicely into a structure of four sets of three verses. And we'll look at those in turn as we begin to unpack the word.

1 Why do the nations rage
And the peoples meditate on a vain thing?
2 The kings of the earth take their stand
And the rulers take counsel together
Against Yahweh and against His Anointed, saying,
3 "Let us tear their fetters apart
And cast away their cords from us!"

4 He who sits in the heavens laughs,
The Lord mocks them.
5 Then He speaks to them in His anger
And terrifies them in His fury, saying,
6 "But as for Me, I have installed My King
Upon Zion, My holy mountain."

7 "I will surely tell of the decree of Yahweh:
He said to Me, 'You are My Son,
Today I have begotten You.

8 'Ask of Me, and I will surely give the nations as Your inheritance,
And the ends of the earth as Your possession.
9 'You shall break them with a rod of iron,
You shall shatter them like a potter's vessel.'"

10 So now, O kings, show insight;
Take warning, O judges of the earth.
11 Serve Yahweh with fear
And rejoice with trembling.
12 Kiss the Son, lest He become angry, and you perish in the way,
For His wrath may soon be kindled.
How blessed are all who take refuge in Him![27]

Do you ever wonder what's going on in our world today? You look around and you see the chaos, the confusion, the conflict, the division, all of those things. You also see men of great ambition and great power who are putting themselves together, as it were, in an effort to try to take control over things. There's this unquenchable desire on the part of some people to have control. And in the midst of that, you look at that and you say to yourself, *what is God up to? What is he doing?* Maybe, *where is he? Are things so far out of control that he's no longer in charge?* Well, there's good news in this psalm because God is certainly in charge.

---

[27] Ps 2 (LSB). Quoted again afterward.

This psalm is an interesting contrast in perspectives because it starts out describing what's happening here on earth. We can look around us and see that what this psalm is saying at the very beginning is certainly going on—that the kings of the earth are taking counsel with each other and setting themselves against God. And what does that mean? That means they are trying to be God themselves. And that causes not only chaos, but misery. So there's a contrast here that's both stunning and it's also encouraging to us because we're looking for a sense of stability at a time when things seem, from our standpoint, to be spiraling out of control.

This psalm will help us make sense out of the world that we live in by giving us a glimpse into heaven. It's not surprising that we see rebellion. This is man's effort to reject the *truth* of God and to reject the *rule* of God. Man wants to do his own thing. And yet we are told here in this psalm that God reigns over all his creation. And it really doesn't matter in the long run how vehemently man tries to fight against him because man cannot defeat God. God has a purpose in this, in case you're wondering, and whether we see it or not, he is already beginning to subdue his enemies under the authority of his anointed King.

Here's a little background on this psalm. It's attributed to David. So it dates from about 3,000 years ago. It's also in the category that's called a *messianic* psalm because it's describing the Messiah. Who is the Messiah?

It is the *anointed* one of God, the one that the Old Testament anticipates over and over as it does in this psalm. A little bit of background on the word. Where do we get the word *Messiah*? The Hebrew word is *mashiyach* and it means *Messiah, Anointed*. So it's translated in this way, *anointed*. And where does that come from? It refers to rubbing with oil. And how does that fit into the equation? It's because when a king or a prophet or a priest was chartered into his office, commissioned into his office, he would be anointed with oil. So this one is called the *anointed*, the *Messiah* or the *mashiyach*. The psalm is referenced several times in the New Testament. It's one of the reasons we can say with great certainty that this is a Messianic psalm because it is applied by the authors of the New Testament to refer directly to Jesus Christ. Christ is the anointed Son who is described in this psalm. And that's how we will be looking at it today.

So as we read this psalm, when it refers to the *Anointed* or the *Son* or *the only begotten* of God, it's referring to Jesus. And this is again, a thousand years before he would come into this world. So we'll take this in four parts. There are four stanzas. I'll read each one and then have some comments on each of the stanzas. We start first with man's *rebellion*. The second stanza is going to give us God's *reaction* to man's rebellion. The third stanza is going to give us the Messiah's *dominion*. And then the fourth stanza is going to be a call to *obedience*, as well as a threat of judgment.

Let's consider first of all, man's rebellion, the first three verses:

1 Why do the nations rage
And the peoples meditate on a vain thing?
2 The kings of the earth take their stand
And the rulers take counsel together
Against Yahweh and against His Anointed, saying,
3 "Let us tear their fetters apart
And cast away their cords from us!"

Here we see figurative language. Quick explanation when it talks about fetters or cords. Other translations will say *yoke*, taking off his yoke. It's referring to God's rightful rule over people, over his creation. Now we notice this begins with a question, and it's kind of a rhetorical question. *Why do the nations rage and the people's plot a vain thing?* And we can think of this in a couple of ways. First of all, the nations, *why do the nations rage?* It's because men are sinners, they're rebels. Ever since the Fall, men have been enemies of God and have been fighting against God. So it's no surprise when we see, even in the present day, men fighting so stridently against God. They do not want to be ruled by God. Secondly, we could also say, that this is a rhetorical question because it exposes the futility of all those efforts—that man is never going to win no matter how hard he strives against his Creator. We notice in these opening verses, it refers to *nations*, to *peoples*, to *kings*, to *rulers*, to all sorts of people. It's as if the whole world is aligning itself and going in league in order to fight against God and against his Messiah. We notice that fallen men will often find common cause in their rebellion. So we see nations, peoples, kings, and rulers all conspiring together. There are a couple of reminders that come to mind here. One is that, in the New Testament, we see that King Herod and Pontius Pilate became friends after having been enemies because they had a common enemy, someone that they commonly scorned, and who was that? That was Jesus. We also can think of how it was in those days that the scribes, the Pharisees, the Sadducees, all conspired together, all conspired with the Roman authorities, all working together to do what? To put Jesus to death.

Something interesting that we notice from this psalm as well. Look at verse two. *They are striving against Yahweh and against his Anointed.* In other words, they know who they're fighting against. They're referring to their fetters and their cords. They know who they're fighting against. This rebellion is neither accidental nor arbitrary. In other words, to use the popular expression, there's no such thing as a rebel without a cause. They know who they're rebelling against. Man's defiance has the effect of suppressing the *truth* of God and rejecting the *law* of God. And here's where we have to observe that man must know what the law of God requires or he wouldn't be fighting so hard against it. Everything he does is a revolt against his Creator. And yet, in the midst of that rebellion and revolt, God is still the ruler over his creation. Those fetters and those cords that the psalmist refers to tell us that God has a rightful claim to rule over his creation. And we see that God wants man's willing obedience. But man uses the freedom that he has, not to put himself into subjection to God, but to rebel against him. Now, rebellion is a plot that's never going to prevail. It may work for a time. When believers are in the midst of it, we may see the chaos and we may say, *it looks like we're losing*. But in fact, God is always winning in spite of how it may appear at the moment.

We also notice that evil men, even when they conspire together, they end up destroying each other. Satan's house is almost inevitably divided against itself in some way. And it's also the case, and we see this often in scripture, that God can send confusion into the camp of his enemies so that they turn their swords against one another. Just when you think that the enemy is going to score a great victory, the enemy's camp is confused and they destroy each other.

Even if the whole creation could be aligned against God, it wouldn't be enough to win. We're told in scripture that *all the nations are like dust on the scales*. That means no matter how powerful they are, how big they are, that you put them on the scale and they cannot even move the needle.

No matter how the plans of men fail, they keep rebelling. Sometimes we look at what's going on and we say, *why do you keep trying to do that? It doesn't work.* Well, that's not the point. We're not going to learn from that when we're in rebellion. We can only continue to rebel unless God changes our hearts. Man's rebellion is driven by a hatred toward God. Man hates God. Man hates God's rule. Man does not want to be ruled by his Creator, and his anger stems from his inability to overthrow God.

We notice, for example—we see this for the first time in the book of Genesis—where man starts making his plans. This expression, *let us . . . let us*, has a recurring theme. And that goes all the way back to that time after the Flood, when men said, *let us make bricks. Let us build a city and a tower. Let us make a name for ourselves.* They're gathering themselves together. And what is God's response in that case? He says, *let us confuse their language.* And by confusing their language, he scatters them abroad and their plans come to nothing. And that's how God can deal very easily with man, even in his rebellion.

The second stanza is God's *reaction.*

> 4 He who sits in the heavens laughs,
> The Lord mocks them.
> 5 Then He speaks to them in His anger
> And terrifies them in His fury, saying,

> 6 "But as for Me, I have installed My King
> Upon Zion, My holy mountain."

And so now in this portion of the psalm, we get a glimpse into heaven after seeing what's happening on earth and seeing the chaos. We now get a glimpse into heaven, what's going on up there. Well, there's a coronation taking place in heaven where Jesus is being placed on the throne and given all power and rule and authority over all the nations. *Can the creature's plans overthrow the Creator?* We find the Bible asking questions like the following. *Has anyone given to God that God should repay him? Has anyone been his counselor? Has anyone taught him the right way?* And the answer, of course, is *no* in all cases. God takes the counsels of the nations, all the wisdom of men, and brings it to nothing. Man's plans, in fact, are so absurd that God laughs in derision, in scorn. Man's wisdom is contemptible in the sight of God because man cannot stand against God. In this stanza, we see God now speaking. Up to this point, the narrator has been speaking, and now God speaks and says, *I have installed my King upon Zion*. So then we ask, if Christ is sitting on his throne in heaven, can man take his place? Is there any place further from man's reach than heaven? And the answer, of course, is *no*, because heaven is that place, as we're told in the gospels, where *thieves do not break in and steal, and where moth and rust do not destroy*.

What response does God have to man's rebellion? Well, God is angry too, as it turns out. But unlike man's anger, God's anger is a righteous anger, and it will be poured out in his wrath against man's rebellion. How, and by what means? We were just told. By the King he is set upon the throne. All power and authority is given to him to subdue the nations, either by grace or by force, if necessary. And those who do not pay homage to the great King will be shattered like a clay pot is shattered by a rod of iron. No one will withstand the day of judgment. None will escape.

The third stanza describes the Messiah's *dominion*. Now this is interesting. And if you're looking at your Bible, notice that in this next set of verses—seven, eight, and nine—this is *Jesus* who is now speaking. He says:

> 7 "I will surely tell of the decree of Yahweh:
> He said to Me, 'You are My Son,
> Today I have begotten You.
> 8 'Ask of Me, and I will surely give the nations as Your inheritance,
> And the ends of the earth as Your possession.
> 9 'You shall break them with a rod of iron,
> You shall shatter them like a potter's vessel.'"

So we see Christ speaking as he says, *Yahweh says to me, you are my Son.* There's clearly a distinction here between the persons. And yet it must be the case that both of the people being referred to—Yahweh and the

Anointed Son—are both God. So even in the Old Testament, we have many indications that God is *one* God in *three* persons. The Son now is the rightful heir of the kingdom. And the kingdom includes everything in heaven and on earth. The nations are his inheritance. But there's a catch, and the catch is that the nations are going to have to be subdued because they are already in rebellion.

Here we can point out that the kings and the rulers of the earth are legitimate powers, but they are all subject to the great King in heaven. All kings and princes and rulers are servants of Yahweh. We're told that *he raises up kings and he brings kings down*. All earthly kings have limited authority, and Yahweh's King rules over them all. And not only in the present, but he will also render judgment on them in the future. So they will either subject themselves to the King of heaven, or as the psalmist warns, they will be crushed by him. And this principle applies to anybody who's in a position of authority. *You serve Christ*. No one rules by his own authority. And to do otherwise is to invite the judgment of God who places you in that position of authority.

In this present age, in spite of the chaos—it's hard to see—but God is subduing the enemies of Christ, though not completely. We have not reached the end of the age yet. And here's where we should say that *this is the day of salvation*. We wonder why the enemies of God are allowed, as it were, to run things their way. It's because God still has a plan for salvation that he's working out. The day of judgment against all who rebel against God will be withheld so that there is time for men to repent—for Christ to continue to build his church until all have been brought in.

The fourth stanza contains the call to *obedience* and also the threat of *judgment*.

> 10 So now, O kings, show insight;
> Take warning, O judges of the earth.
> 11 Serve Yahweh with fear
> And rejoice with trembling.
> 12 Kiss the Son, lest He become angry, and you perish in the way,
> For His wrath may soon be kindled. . . .

And finally, a benediction:

> How blessed are all who take refuge in Him!

There are the choices. We either set ourselves against God, as the men described at the beginning of this psalm, or we take refuge in him as we see here at the end. Those who oppose God and his Messiah will surely be destroyed. Those who serve God and his Messiah will surely be blessed. It's one or the other. There's no third option. And here we have to say that man does not make his own way of salvation. He either receives the gift of salvation that's been provided to him by God through Christ, or he must perish according to his own works. We're reminded that the broad road is the one that leads to destruction, and that only the narrow road is the one that leads to eternal life. Man in his rebellion bears a yoke of sin and of judgment. And it's one that he cannot bear on his own. He must lay it aside and take up the yoke that God has prepared for him because God has made a way out. Obedience to the Son frees man from the bondage to his sin. And God takes no delight in the death of the wicked. On the contrary, the scripture tells us, *there is rejoicing in heaven at the repentance of a single sinner*.

Now listen to what the Messiah says in the New Testament.

> "Come to Me, all who are weary and heavy-laden, and I will give you rest. Take My yoke upon you and learn from Me, for I am gentle and humble in heart, and YOU WILL FIND REST FOR YOUR SOULS. For My yoke is easy and My burden is light."[28]

Have you come to Christ for rest from the guilt and shame of your sin? Will you lay down your yoke of sin and take up the yoke of grace? Will you give homage to the Son so that he turns his wrath away from you? Will you live as a servant of the living God and of his anointed King?

---

[28] Matt 11:28-30 (LSB).

To summarize our thoughts here, this psalm reminds us that man's rebellion is nothing new. The testimony of scripture is that the last days in which we live will be *perilous times*. But it also reminds us that Christ reigns in heaven and that God is subduing all his enemies in part by bringing them into the kingdom of Christ through salvation. The world will one day be put right, just as it was in the beginning. And Christ will return on a future day to judge the whole world in righteousness according to all the thoughts and the intentions of the heart. In the meantime, we can take encouragement and live confidently in this present evil age because Christ reigns in heaven. And we have the assurance of a place in heaven where peace and righteousness reign forever and ever.

So finally friends, are you plotting a vain thing by your rejection of God and Christ? Do you think your strength will prevail against the one who shatters the nations like clay pots? Then kiss the Son and thereby there will be rejoicing in heaven. Remember that *blessed are all those who take refuge in him*. So, *delight yourself in the Lord and he will give you the desires of your heart*. Put your trust in the Lord Jesus Christ, both now and forever. Under the shadow of his wings, you will find safety from the storm of destruction.

Jesus says this:

> "For not even the Father judges anyone, but He has given all judgment to the Son, so that all will honor the Son even as they honor the Father. He who does not honor the Son does not honor the Father who sent Him.
>
> "Truly, truly, I say to you, he who hears My word, and believes Him who sent Me, has eternal life, and does not come into judgment, but has passed out of death into life."[29]

Amen.

Let's pray. Father, we ask that you would apply these words to our hearts and our minds today. Bring any to salvation who need it, and give encouragement to all who have it. I pray these things in Jesus' name. Amen.

[29] John 5:22-24 (LSB)

Christ the Priestly King (Psalm 110)

May 28, 2023

Today we will give our attention to the 110th Psalm:

1 Yahweh says to my Lord [Jesus]:
"Sit at My right hand
Until I put Your enemies as a footstool for Your feet."

2 Yahweh will stretch forth Your strong scepter from Zion, saying,
"Have dominion in the midst of Your enemies."

3 Your people will offer themselves freely in the day of Your power;
In the splendor of holiness, from the womb of the dawn,
The dew of Your youthfulness will be Yours.

4 Yahweh has sworn and will not change His mind,
"You are a priest forever
According to the order of Melchizedek."

5 The Lord [Yahweh] is at Your right hand;
He will crush kings in the day of His anger.

6 He will render justice among the nations,
He will fill them with corpses,
He will crush the head that is over the wide earth.

7 He will drink from the brook by the wayside;
Therefore He will lift up His head.[30]

---

[30] Ps 110 (LSB). Quoted again afterward. References to *Jesus* (v. 1) and *Yahweh* (v. 5) added.

This is a Psalm of David. It was written about 3,000 years ago. It was written 1,000 years before Christ. And it also takes us back 1,000 years before David with this reference to someone called Melchizedek. And then it ties all the way through the New Testament as we will see when we look more closely at this.

Let me start with this thought. You're familiar with the expression when it says that someone has a right-hand man. What does that mean? It's been a common saying for many years. It refers to someone who is of considerable influence and considerable importance, doesn't it? When we talk about someone who's *at so-and-so's right hand*. It's never more true, of course, than it is in regard to the Son of God, who sits at the right hand of God the Father. If we were having a party and seating people at the dinner table, if you sit at the right hand of the host, you occupy a place of honor among the guests. But what does it mean if you sit at the right hand of the king? It means not only a place of *honor*, but a place where you exercise *rule*, you have *authority*.

So we look at the world today and we wonder, who's really in charge of this mess? What's really going on? We see princes and presidents and politicians who are all jostling for supremacy. We see confusion everywhere. It's in the air and we're surrounded by an assortment of deceptions that draw us away from the truth. We live in a time where fear is often gripping our society. We're constantly being told about the threats around us that are going to endanger all of our lives if we don't do something right away. The irony is that men are made to fear death. But in the meanwhile, men seem to forget God and seem to forget the one they *should* fear—who not only can destroy the body, but we're told can destroy both body and soul. So what is going on in this world? Why are there such divisions? And how is it all going to end?

If we like movies or stories, we're always curious about how it's going to end. And this psalm gives us a picture, not only of the current state of affairs, but of how these things will all come to a conclusion at God's hand. This psalm is going to help us answer some very difficult questions like these. God *reigns*, but man is in a state of *rebellion*. So we see that the present age that we live in is a battle between good and evil. We see that evidence around us all the time. Nevertheless—and it may be more difficult to see—but God is extending his kingdom through the gospel of grace even as men continue to rebel against him, because this is the age of repentance. God will soon judge the world and bring it into total conformity to his perfect law to set all things right. And on that day, there are none who will be able to stand against his purposes. And that this psalm gives us a picture 3,000 years ago of Jesus Christ as God's right hand man who will rule and reign over his creation. And we saw last time in Psalm 2 that he rules from heaven, from heavenly Zion. None can resist his power in the long run. And those who will not honor the Son with their obedience will be destroyed by the rod of iron.

There are many similarities between this psalm and Psalm 2, which we considered last time. Again, it's a Psalm of David. It's attributed to David in the text, and it's also the case that Jesus himself, referring to this psalm, says, *David said*. So we know that it's David who is speaking through this psalm. It's a messianic psalm, meaning that it's referring to that Anointed one, that chosen one, the one who will carry out God's rule, and reign over this creation.

The first verse of this psalm, where it says, *Yahweh says to my Lord, sit at my right hand until I put your enemies as a footstool to your feet*, is quoted repeatedly in the New Testament, at least 27 times. So it must be of some importance if that particular verse is repeated so many times. Not only this gives us a clue about the importance, but it also is going to give us a basis for understanding what it means when scripture is referencing other parts of scripture. Jesus himself quotes from this psalm in a confrontation that he has with the Pharisees. And this psalm references an important historical event that we find in the book of Genesis. And so it has the effect of tying something that happened way back in the book of Genesis, a thousand years earlier, with something in the present and something that will happen in the future.[31]

We're going to consider this psalm in four parts. Let's see if you can pick up on a recurring theme. First is Christ's *kingship*. Secondly is Christ's *army*. Third is Christ's *priesthood*. And lastly is Christ's *victory*. Notice a pattern there? This is a psalm about Christ. It's also a demonstration of how Christ is to be found in all the scriptures. It's not just the New Testament where you find him, but it's in all the Bible. And you'll recall that, on the road to Emmaus after the resurrection, what was it he said to those disciples? That everything written in the law of Moses and in the prophets had to be fulfilled. And he opened the scriptures to them on that occasion.

First we're going to consider Christ's *kingship*, the first two verses.

> 1 Yahweh says to my Lord [Jesus]:
> "Sit at My right hand
> Until I put Your enemies as a footstool for Your feet."
>
> 2 Yahweh will stretch forth Your strong scepter from Zion, saying,
> "Have dominion in the midst of Your enemies."

[31] Referring to a thousand years before the psalm was written—2,000 B.C.—and the advent of Christ that would occur a thousand years after the psalm was written.

So again, who is speaking? This is David who is speaking. David is relating something that by divine inspiration was revealed to him, a conversation that took place between God the Father and God the Son. It's the case that if we see one person speaking to another, that there must be two persons involved in that conversation. And so we get an important clue from this psalm that the person of God exists in more than one person, or that—I should say—the Trinity of God exists in more than one person.

Let's start to unpack this a little bit. It says, *rule in the midst of your enemies*. Who are God's enemies? If God has enemies, who are they? And when did the war begin? Well, Genesis answers that question for us, because if we go back to the Garden of Eden, what do we find? We find a man created in his perfection, and we find a law given to him by God, and then we find the Serpent coming onto the scene, speaking deception, and Adam and Eve falling into disobedience and bringing sin into the world. And it's at that time we are told there is now *enmity* or warfare between the offspring of the Serpent and the offspring of the woman. So we're engaged in warfare and have been ever since the very beginning and will be until the end.

What does it mean when it says, *I will put your enemies as a footstool for your feet*? That's an odd kind of expression, but it refers to the idea that a conquering king will literally put his foot on his conquered enemy as a way of showing that he's been defeated. So we have that picture for us in this psalm. Even in the Garden, we have an interesting picture of the idea between *head* and *feet*. And what is it? We're told that the Seed of the woman will crush the head of the Serpent under his foot. As scripture unfolds, we learn that the Seed of the woman will be a descendant of David. So it's important that David is writing this psalm. He's referring in some way to someone who will be among his descendants when he refers to *my Lord*.

Back in Genesis, at the very end of Genesis, before Jacob dies, he gives us this important prophecy. He says, *the scepter*—which is that symbol of power or rule—*will not depart from Judah, nor the ruler's staff from between his feet, until Shiloh comes. And to him shall be the obedience of the peoples*.[32] In other words, there's going to be some figure coming from the tribe of Judah who will hold that rod of power and will bring the whole world into subjection under that. This descendant will be a man, but we also see that he's going to be more than a man, because he will also be God, the Messiah, who is God's chosen Son to rule.

Jesus quotes verse 1 from Psalm 110 in the New Testament. In fact, he's using it to pose a riddle to his critics. As you know, the scribes and the

---

[32] Gen 49:10 (LSB).

Pharisees were always trying to confront him and to catch him in some error. So we have this narrative:

> Now while the Pharisees were gathered together, Jesus asked them a question, saying, "What do you think about the Christ, whose son is He?" They said to Him, "The son of David." He said to them, "Then how does David in the Spirit call Him 'Lord,' saying,
>
> 'THE LORD SAID TO MY LORD,
> "SIT AT MY RIGHT HAND,
> UNTIL I PUT YOUR ENEMIES BENEATH YOUR FEET"'?
>
> Therefore, if David calls Him 'Lord,' how is He his son?" And no one was able to answer Him a word, nor did anyone dare from that day on to ask Him another question.[33]

Here's Jesus using the first verse of this psalm to confront his enemies over the question of who was the Christ. We know from the New Testament that David was speaking here of someone who would come after him, of one of his offspring. The question then is, how could a *son* of David be greater than his father? That's not the normal order of things. And the answer is that it would only be the case if that son, that *son of David*, as Jesus is often referred to, would have not only a human nature, but a divine nature. Again, here in verse two, we see the scepter as a symbol of power in the hands of the king. In Psalm 2 (last time) we saw

[33] Matt 22:41-46 (LSB).

this as a *rod of iron*, that symbol of power that would crush the nations like clay pots. The one who holds the scepter is obviously the one who has the power to rule.

In this first verse, God is promising to subdue all the enemies of his Messiah and put them under his feet—that is, in the place of humility and subjection. And the reference to Zion refers to that heavenly palace of the King. It is the heavenly Jerusalem. And remember, we had a little glimpse into heaven when we looked at Psalm 2. Christ is ruling, quote, *in the midst of his enemies*. And that's referring to a spiritual dominion that works within and around earthly powers. There is no border that can stop the gospel. The promise of the gospel, in fact, is that it will reach men of every nation, tribe, tongue, and people. That the church of Jesus Christ, if you want to put it this way, would infiltrate every earthly political jurisdiction. There is no border and no power that can ever stop it.

Let's now look at verse three, Christ's army. It says:

> 3 Your people will offer themselves freely in the day of Your power;
> In the splendor of holiness, from the womb of the dawn,
> The dew of Your youthfulness will be Yours.

Here's where I have to say that this verse presents a little bit of difficulty of interpretation because the psalms are poetry. And so we have poetic language and figurative language that is used at times. And sometimes the manner of speaking is unusual to us. We don't recognize it. We use figures of speech ourselves all the time, but someone in a different country might find our figures of speech to be very strange. So we'll have to see if we can understand more clearly what this verse is saying.

The first part of the verse is easy enough because it describes God's people in terms of them being a freewill offering. They are giving themselves without reservation. It's an idea that we see echoed in places like Romans 12, where Paul says, *I exhort you brothers by the mercies of God to present your bodies as a sacrifice—living, holy, and pleasing to* God, *which is your spiritual service of worship.*[34] So there's nothing exceptional about the idea of bringing yourself as the offering to God. You're placing yourself into the service of the king as a slave for him to use however he pleases. And here I would add that this is more than just volunteering for a job because it's a recognition that you owe your life to the one who has saved you. It is a permanent office that you undertake in service to Christ. The Christian life is described in just this way. And it's because the King, Christ, has freed us from our slavery to sin, so that we now become slaves of righteousness. He says, *you were bought*, Paul says this, *you were bought with a price: therefore glorify* God *in your body.*[35] We have been purchased.

[34] Rom 12:1 (LSB).

[35] 1 Cor 6:20 (LSB).

Here's where another translation could be a little helpful to us. So I'm going to quote from the *New International Version* (NIV) of this verse. Listen to how much different the verse sounds.

> 3 Your troops will be willing
> on your day of battle.
> Arrayed in holy splendor,
> your young men will come to you
> like dew from the morning's womb.[36]

This gives us a much different picture. These are describing not just those who have volunteered into the service of God, but those who are *arrayed for battle*. And oddly enough, they're not wearing battle gear, they're wearing priestly robes.

The New Testament uses military language in describing our spiritual warfare. Again, that goes all the way back to the Garden of Eden. *We fight against powers and principalities in the heavenly realms*. And therefore our weapons are to be spiritual weapons, especially the sword of the word of God, which is the gospel. Our spiritual battle is actually a rescue operation because we have to raid the enemy's camp and bring men out of the power of darkness by the power of the gospel. That idea of *the dew of the morning* is poetically describing an uncountable multitude of

[36] Ps 110:3 (NIV).

soldiers in the army of Christ. And those who are new are renewed every morning and they glisten like dew in the power of God. And what was interesting is just this morning, looking out my office window where the sun had not yet come around the side of the house, and seeing the drops of dew on all the new green blades of grass. This verse took a special meaning just at that very moment.

The *willingness* of our submission is the essence of what it means to be holy. We're placing ourselves into the service of the King. It honors him as King when we place ourselves in obedience to him. And the funny thing is that as we do, we become more like him. We understand that God's army in this age is his church, and that his church reaches the ends of the earth in this age of grace. Again, there are no boundaries that men can create that will stop the progress of the church of Jesus Christ and the power of the gospel.

I'm going to share you one more interpretation of this verse. This is from the Baptist preacher William Graham Scroggie from the mid 20th century. This is his paraphrase of the verse. And so he's added—let's say—a little bit of color to help us hopefully understand more clearly what this is.

He says:

> Thy people shall offer themselves as free-will offerings in the day of Thy prowess [Thy power], when Thine does muster Thine army for battle.
>
> And they shall come clad in holy garments, in priestly vestments, for Thy soldiers are also priests; and as dew is born of its mother in the morning, so Thy army shall come to Thee numerous, fresh, bright, and powerful.[37]

That's a very interesting exposition of that verse.

Let's talk now about Christ's *priesthood*, verse four. This strange figure that we saw first in Genesis now shows up again.

> 4 Yahweh has sworn and will not change His mind,
> "You are a priest forever
> According to the order of Melchizedek."

And if you search your Bible, you will find that there are just a few references to Melchizedek. And at the end of that search, you will discover that you don't know much more about Melchizedek than you did when you started.

Let's start first with the idea that *God swore an oath*. That ought to strike us as interesting and important because when God speaks, he always

---

[37] Scroggie, *The Psalms*, p. 85.

speaks the truth. Why would he need to speak and add an oath to it? And in this case, that the oath of God gives us greater confidence that he will accomplish what he is determined to do. And the reminder that no earthly power can overcome it. So in times like ours of utter chaos, we need the assurance that God is still at work and has *not changed his mind*, that in spite of how things may look, the victory of Christ is drawing closer by the day.

Now back to Melchizedek. We first encounter him in the book of Genesis in chapter 14. This is right after Abraham defeats a coalition of invading kings. We recall that Abraham's nephew Lot was among those who were living in Sodom when it was overthrown and he's one of the ones who's been carried away by the invaders. So Abraham determines to muster a small army of only a few hundred and go after these kings and defeat them and rescue all the people and restore all the property. Here's how the narrative goes.

> Then after he [Abram] came back from striking down Chedorlaomer and the kings who were with him, the king of Sodom went out to meet him at the valley of Shaveh (that is, the King's Valley).
>
> And Melchizedek king of Salem brought out bread and wine; now he was a priest of God Most High. Then he blessed him and said,

> "Blessed be Abram of God Most High,
> Possessor of heaven and earth;
> And blessed be God Most High,
> Who has delivered your enemies into your hand."
>
> Then he gave him a tenth of all.[38]

We have God here being referred to as God Most High, *El Elyon*, which is a title that we often see in the Bible, and several times in this passage. It's used four times just in this passage. And from this, we know that this king, this high priest, was worshiping the true God. He was no idol worshiper. He knew the true God. And yet we also can see that he was not a descendant of Abraham. In fact, we don't know who he's descended from and we don't know who came after him. We have no information. And that's a little ironic because, if you read your Bible, you know that there are often genealogies, long lists of people who are fathers and sons and grandsons and so on, generation after generation, and even down to the New Testament, where we see in the beginning of the Gospel of Matthew, a genealogy that shows us that Christ is both a son of Abraham and a son of David. So those ideas of knowing your ancestry are very important in the Jewish narrative. And yet this Melchizedek shows up and we have no idea where he came from, who his daddy was, as we would say. We don't know who came after him. He appears very mysteriously on the scene at this time. And that's literally just about all

[38] Gen 14:17-20 (LSB).

we know about him. He shows up without any explanation, but he is described as a genuine priest of God. And if he's a priest of God, that means that God must have called him to that office in some special way, because no one takes the office of a priest without God's authority. His rank is demonstrated by the fact that the greater blesses the lesser. Melchizedek blessed Abraham. What does that tell us? Melchizedek was greater than Abraham, and yet Abraham was the father of the Jewish people and would become so over time. So, very interesting how this mysterious figure of Melchizedek is prefiguring Christ who would come 2,000 years later. Melchizedek was a man whose calling provided a picture of the future Messiah and a gospel that would reach not just the Jewish people, but all the nations. And though he was mysterious, he was nevertheless just a man. He was not a divine figure. He was intended for just a unique priesthood that would be pointing forward to God's Messiah.

This is part of what the New Testament has to say about him.

> [Melchizedek] . . . was first of all, by the translation of his name, king of righteousness, and then also king of Salem, which is king of peace. Without father, without mother, without genealogy, having neither beginning of days nor end of life, but made like the Son of God, he remains a priest continually.[39]

[39] Heb 7:2-3 (LSB).

And although he was a man in this mysterious way, he is prefiguring the Christ who will come.

This idea of Salem as a city quite possibly refers to ancient Jerusalem. And if so, then it only strengthens the idea that he is prefiguring Christ because Jerusalem becomes that place from which the nation of Israel will be ruled, and even called *Zion*.

Now what is meant by *the order of Melchizedek?* Think of this in terms of a certain pattern, that the priesthood of Christ would follow a similar pattern. It would not follow the pattern that is going to be given to Moses in the Law, where the priests are all part of the line of Levi. The priesthood of Christ will be not only of a different order, but a *higher* order, which is directly from God and which will make it a better priesthood and a lasting priesthood, *forever*, as David says here. So we see the picture of a permanent priesthood which in that respect, none have come before and none have come after that are like it. The priesthood of the Levites was temporary for a certain time in the history of Israel. And that would only serve to point to what I'm calling the *forever high priest*.

It's also the case that this priesthood of the Messiah is connected also to the office of a *king*. And that's a very strange thing, that those two offices should be combined. It's a departure from the Mosaic law. As we saw from the prophecy in the book of Genesis by Jacob, the kingship would come through the tribe of Judah and the priesthood would, of course, come through the tribe of Levi, and those were kept separate. So in the administration of Israel, kings and priests were always kept separate. And if a king tried to perform the functions of a priest, he very quickly got himself into trouble because those things were not to be done.

The idea of a priest is one of an *intercessor*, someone who stands between man and God. We could think of this like a lawyer, an attorney, who goes representing that client and standing before the judge on behalf of the client and representing him to the judge, petitioning on his behalf. The priests of old interceded with daily sacrifices, whereas this *forever high priest* will give himself as the one perfect offering for his people for all time and fulfill all that's required in the law.

Now consider, as we bring this to a conclusion, *the victory of Christ*, these last three verses.

> 5 The Lord [Yahweh] is at Your right hand;
> He will crush kings in the day of His anger.
>
> 6 He will render justice among the nations,
> He will fill them with corpses,
> He will crush the head that is over the wide earth.

7 He will drink from the brook by the wayside;
Therefore He will lift up His head.

There's a day coming when the full wrath of God is going to be unleashed on any who still reject him. And if kings will not stand against the judgment in that day, then no one else will stand either. The conquest of the Messiah will overthrow kings and nations and peoples everywhere. It will be a day of violent conquest. The language is very graphic at this point. But we can think of the book of Revelation in the way that it also paints a graphic picture of violence of such that the blood of Christ's enemies will flow like a river in that day. Until then though, the day of salvation is at hand and the gospel commands all men to repent and to believe in Christ for salvation. We are reminded of where the conflict started, with that ancient battle between Christ and Satan. Here now, at this time, the Seed of the woman fatally crushes the head of the serpent, and the victor will lift up his head, and the vanquished will never raise his head again.

During David's reign as king, he desired to build a house for God. It was not a task that fell to him. It instead fell to Solomon, his son, after him. But from that time, from the time of Moses until the time of David, God dwelt in a tent called the Tabernacle. Now David desires to do something that is a noble thing, to build God a house. But God denies David the opportunity to do that, and instead gives him a remarkable promise.

David says, *I want to build a house for you.* And God says, *No, but I'm going to build a house for you.* And he's using figurative language to mean that there will be a descendant from David that will reign on the throne until the Messiah comes. And when the Messiah comes as the son of David, he will reign on that throne of Judah forever. The scripture says, *your house and your kingdom shall endure before Me forever; your throne shall be established forever.*[40] Christ is the house that God promised to build for David. And even now he is reigning from heaven and will continue to reign while God subdues his enemies.

As we bring this to a close, we see in this psalm a fuller picture of the person and the work of the Messiah. He is both king and high priest, and he ever lives to make intercession for his people. He promises that all of his enemies—and all of our enemies—will be overcome, and that we will reign with him forever in that heavenly Zion.

Consider the following. Have you given yourself body and soul to Christ as a freewill offering? Have you placed your trust in him to make payment for your sin as God's *forever high priest*? Is Christ your mediator or is he your judge? Will you humbly place yourself at his feet in obedience, or will you be trampled underfoot in your rebellion? Christ the Lord has offered himself up to God to pay the penalty for sin. All that you must do

---

[40] 2 Sam 7:16 (LSB)

is believe that he will save you and deliver you into the kingdom of heaven. If you fully trust him, you will be as that morning dew, glistening in the dawn of new life as you reflect the power and the glory of your Savior. You will one day then take your place with Christ on his throne to inherit the nations and to rule over them in righteousness with him. In the meantime, in this age, we can take courage because Messiah reigns and God is subduing all of his enemies and ours to the glory of God.

Amen.

Let's pray. Father, as we consider this beautiful word in Psalm 110, we ask that you would apply it to each of our hearts. That you would bring us willingly as servants of the great High King and High Priest. Make us part of the treasure that will be part of his inheritance in heaven. And we ask that you would be with us in the time that we have here, that we would take courage in the promises of God and know that the oath of God can never ever change. You will accomplish all that you have determined to do, in spite of all the resistance of all the nations. And we pray these things in Christ's name. Amen.

Christ the Great Shepherd of the Sheep

(Psalm 23)

June 18, 2023

The passage that I've chosen today, in keeping with the psalms that we've been looking at, is a little bit of a daunting task. I'll tell you why in just a minute, but you'll think, *why is this a problem?* Because it's probably one that you already know, and that is the 23rd Psalm. And today I'm going to read it in the *King James Version*. I wouldn't be surprised if many of you, like me, first learned this psalm in the *King James Version*. So, in keeping with what we already may have hidden in our hearts, I'm going to read that version today. Six verses.

> 1 The LORD is my shepherd; I shall not want.
> 2 He maketh me to lie down in green pastures: he leadeth me beside the still waters.
> 3 He restoreth my soul: he leadeth me in the paths of righteousness for his name's sake.
> 4 Yea, though I walk through the valley of the shadow of death, I will fear no evil: for thou art with me; thy rod and thy staff they comfort me.
> 5 Thou preparest a table before me in the presence of mine enemies: thou anointest my head with oil; my cup runneth over.
> 6 Surely goodness and mercy shall follow me all the days of my life: and I will dwell in the house of the LORD for ever.[41]

---

[41] Ps 23 (KJV). Quoted again afterward.

If I were smarter, I would just stop there because what am I going to add to that? And that's what makes this a little daunting because it's such a familiar passage. Frankly, I don't want to ruin it for you. So I hope that as we look at this today, it will deepen your love and appreciation for this psalm. This is also called *The Shepherd's Psalm*. The title that I'll use for today is *Christ, the Great Shepherd of the Sheep*. We're going to learn something about that great Shepherd today.

This is perhaps the best known and best loved passage in the whole Bible. And if there's one psalm that you learned by heart at some point, it was probably this one. It's short and it's simple enough that a child can learn it. And yet this psalm is deep enough to give us comfort through the whole course of our lives, even to the very end. And it's the kind of passage that can grow more and more precious to us over time, especially as we see the truth of these verses unfolding in the course of our lives. It's the kind of text (you might say) that is proved best in hindsight as you look back over the course of your Christian life and see how the Shepherd has guided you throughout all your life. F.B. Meyer calls it *one of the most holy places in the temple of scripture*. And it's the kind of psalm that helps us fix our gaze upon the Shepherd and not look so much at ourselves—that we are the beneficiaries of his work. It's the kind of psalm that even if we've never been shepherds, we have an intuitive understanding of it. We all have some notion of what it means for a shepherd to keep watch over his sheep. And we also connect this pastoral imagery of the psalm with many other parts of scripture. And we'll look at some of those today. God is often described as a *shepherd* and his people are described as *the sheep of his pasture* or his *flock*.

The task I have today is to strengthen your love and appreciation, not just for this psalm, but for the Shepherd who's described in it. So we'll think of four questions today. First of all, *who is the Shepherd?* Secondly, *what does he do?* Thirdly, *what result does it produce?* And lastly, *how do I make him my Shepherd?*

We'll start with a little background. This is a Psalm of David. It's not messianic like some of the psalms that we've looked at here, but we could call it a pastoral psalm. It's pointing to Christ as the Good Shepherd who cares for his sheep, even when it costs him his life, which it does. It was written 3,000 years ago and it's been a source of comfort for believers for all of those 3,000 years. It does not promise an easy life, but what it does promise is God's care in the midst of life and in the midst of our troubles. David probably wrote this later in his life. We don't know exactly when, but it seems to be written by someone who can look back on the course of his life and see how God has been his Shepherd throughout his life.

David himself was a shepherd when he was a boy. You probably know that. And shepherding was a pretty lousy job. It usually ended up being assigned to the youngest son in the family. It was both dirty and dangerous. We'll recall that David had to be called from the field keeping his sheep when Samuel came at God's behest to anoint the next king of Israel. Let me look at that passage in 1 Samuel 16. It says:

> Thus Jesse made seven of his sons pass before Samuel. But Samuel said to Jesse, "Yahweh has not chosen these." And Samuel said to Jesse, "Are these all the young men?" And he said, "There remains yet the youngest, and behold, he is shepherding the sheep." Then Samuel said to Jesse, "Send and bring him, for we will not turn around until he comes here." So he sent and brought him in. Now he was ruddy, with beautiful eyes and a handsome appearance. And Yahweh said, "Arise, anoint him, for this is he." Then Samuel took the horn of oil and anointed him in the midst of his brothers; and the Spirit of Yahweh came mightily upon David from that day forward.[42]

Unlike his eldest brothers, three of whom, the three eldest who served in the army, David was not a trained warrior, but he was skilled at defending his sheep. And so we see in the very next chapter, 1 Samuel 17, there's this incident with a big guy named Goliath. He was able to face this giant because of his skill. And I want to share that passage of 1 Samuel 17 with you as well.

---

[42] 1 Sam 16:10-13a (LSB).

> And David said to Saul, "Let no man's heart fail on account of him; your servant will go and fight with this Philistine." Then Saul said to David, "You are not able to go against this Philistine to fight with him; for you are but a youth while he has been a warrior from his youth." But David said to Saul, "Your servant was shepherding his father's sheep. And a lion and a bear would come and take a lamb from the flock, and I would go out after it and strike it and rescue the lamb from its mouth. Then it rose up against me, and I would seize it by its beard and strike it down and put it to death. Your servant has struck down both the lion and the bear; and this uncircumcised Philistine will be like one of them, since he has reproached the battle lines of the living God." And David said, "Yahweh, who delivered me from the hand of the lion and from the hand of the bear, He will deliver me from the hand of this Philistine." And Saul said to David, "Go, and may Yahweh be with you."[43]

And so he bravely went out to face the Philistine. And what did he have to fight him with? A sling and some sling stones. And this was a common tool of the shepherd. The shepherd typically would have a rod and a staff and perhaps a sling. And he would use the sling among other things to defend his flock against attackers. So David goes out with the tools of his trade, faces Goliath, strikes him down and kills him with his own sword. So part of what we see in the shepherd's job is to care for the wellbeing of his sheep, including their defense against predators like lions and bears and against poachers who might attack them or steal them.

---

[43] 1 Sam 17:32-37 (LSB).

Now we know that David became, as we would say, an overnight sensation for his bravery in fighting and killing the giant. And in David, we get a glimpse of what a skilled and brave shepherd can do. It might be a menial kind of job, but it requires considerable skill and considerable attention. And so it is this man who served as a *shepherd* in his youth who is now looking back on his life and writing a psalm as a *sheep*. He's writing in order to talk about the Great Shepherd who has been *his* shepherd.

Let's start with the very first verse and ask the question, *who is this Shepherd?* It says, *the Lord is my Shepherd.* So it's a poetic description of our Great Shepherd. It is a window that allows us to see him more fully. We see that he is a meek and lowly man, but this Shepherd we're talking about here is also God, and he will do far more than just keep his sheep. We know that he is also the Commander of the armies of the Lord. He himself is a great warrior. And as we have seen in some of the other psalms we've looked at, this Shepherd is also an anointed King, and he's also a Great High Priest. We don't want to miss the important point that he is the subject of this psalm and that his sheep are the object of it. In other words, the shepherd is the one who is in the foreground, not the sheep. And when we read and meditate on this psalm, it should always focus our attention on him. We know as the shepherd, he has to be near his sheep at all times. Being a shepherd is an around-the-clock job. We also know the shepherd must put the safety and the comfort of his flock above his own concerns. He may often have to risk his own life in protecting his flock.

If we go back to the book of Genesis, we find that Jacob was also a shepherd. And during twenty years in the employ of his uncle Laban, he served as a shepherd. And I'd like to share a portion of that passage with you just to give you an idea of what he had to deal with as a shepherd. He says to his uncle Laban:

> These twenty years I have been with you; your ewes and your female goats have not miscarried, nor have I eaten the rams of your flocks. That which was torn of beasts I did not bring to you; I bore the loss of it myself. You required it of my hand whether stolen by day or stolen by night. Thus I was: by day the heat consumed me and the frost by night, and my sleep fled from my eyes.[44]

A very difficult job and one that gives very little rest. And why? Because you can't take your eyes off the sheep. Now there's an affinity that develops between the sheep and the shepherd. He cares for his flock somewhat as if they were his children. He knows them all by name. And we also know that the sheep know the voice of their shepherd and they will follow only the voice of their own shepherd. Now God is known to his sheep by his personal name, *Yahweh*. It doesn't come out in the King

---

[44] Gen 31:38-40 (LSB).

James translation, but that's what we see at the very beginning of this psalm. This name is important because it tells us that he has made a way for us to be in relationship to him through his covenant promises. And some of the benefits of those promises are expressed in this psalm. In the Old Testament, this *Yahweh* is called *the Shepherd of Israel*. We read things like this, that *he leads his people like a flock. He tends his flock like a shepherd. He seeks his sheep as a shepherd seeks his flock. He gathers Israel as a shepherd gathers his scattered sheep*. And then as we come to the New Testament, we see that it's very clear that this Shepherd of God's people is none other than Jesus Christ. The apostle Peter calls him by the titles of *Chief Shepherd* and *overseer of your souls*. He tends both to our physical and our spiritual care.

Jesus says this:

> "I am the good shepherd, and I know My own and My own know Me, even as the Father knows Me and I know the Father; and I lay down My life for the sheep."[45]

Paradoxically, the Shepherd is also called the *Lamb* who will be slain as a sacrifice for the sin of his people. In the book of Revelation, he is described as a King and a Shepherd and a Lamb, all at the same time. Listen to this passage:

---

[45] John 10:14-15 (LSB).

"He who sits on the throne. . .

That's the *king*.

> ". . .will dwell over them. THEY WILL HUNGER NO LONGER, NOR THIRST ANYMORE; NOR WILL THE SUN BEAT DOWN ON THEM, NOR ANY HEAT; for the Lamb at the center of the throne will shepherd them and will guide them to springs of the water of life. And God WILL WIPE EVERY TEAR FROM THEIR EYES."[46]

We see this Great Shepherd's ministry is both now and forever. It's all sufficient for our present needs, and it's also leading us through this life towards a glorious future.

Consider now our second question. *What does the shepherd do?* These are the first five verses. Let me reread them.

> 1 The LORD is my shepherd; I shall not want.
> 2 He maketh me to lie down in green pastures: he leadeth me beside the still waters.
> 3 He restoreth my soul: he leadeth me in the paths of righteousness for his name's sake.
> 4 Yea, though I walk through the valley of the shadow of death, I will fear no evil: for thou art with me; thy rod and thy staff they comfort me.

---

[46] Rev 7:15b-17 (LSB).

> 5 Thou preparest a table before me in the presence of mine enemies: thou anointest my head with oil; my cup runneth over.

Can you think of all the things that he's describing that he is doing for his people in those short verses? We could ask the question this way: *what does it mean for him to be my shepherd?* Well, if he's the shepherd, then I must be the *sheep*. And sheep are peculiar animals, perhaps more than any other kind of livestock. They need the most care and the most attention. They're always prone to wander off and to get into trouble. Does that ring any bells? Sheep are the most vulnerable to predators, which means they need a protector. And here's how I might describe it, that they're a lot like children who have to be watched all the time. And if you remember what it was like to have a three-year-old in the house, you do not take your eye off of a three-year-old, not even for twenty seconds. So *like sheep, we've all gone astray*. And we will be lost forever if the shepherd does not come and get us and bring us back into the flock.

When that passage says that *we like sheep have gone astray, each one has turned to his own way*, it's not saying we just randomly wandered off. It means that we decided we were going to do things our own way. And inevitably when that happens, we get ourselves into trouble and our Shepherd has to come and rescue us from our own foolishness.

There are at least four things that our Shepherd has to do for us. He *pities* us because we are fallen creatures and we need his mercy. He *protects* us because we face many dangers, both physical and spiritual. He *provides* for us because we have many needs, both physical and spiritual. And he also *chastises* us because in our weakness, we must be trained and disciplined.

Let's look at verse one more closely where it says, *the Lord is my shepherd, I shall not want*. Here's a simple statement of what we would describe as *cause and effect*. Because God is my Shepherd, therefore we will lack nothing needful. The conclusion follows the premise, to use the logical expression. If God is my Shepherd, he will provide everything that is needful. And we could say that this psalm starts with the bottom line. That's the most important thing that we can take from this, that he will provide everything that we need. So, what follows in the next verses has a lot of details about exactly what he does. Because he is the Creator and sustainer of all things, God is certainly very well equipped to provide for our needs, and no one knows us better than he does in exactly what we may need. The Bible says it this way, that *those who seek the Lord lack no good thing. He withholds nothing from those who walk uprightly. He satisfies the longing of the soul.* That *those who seek his kingdom and his righteousness first will have all their necessary provision added to them*: food, clothes, shelter, and the rest. The apostle Paul assures his readers that *his God will supply every need of theirs*, both material and spiritual.

Here's an interesting little twist on this psalm where it says, *I shall not want*. There's actually something that's even a little better than that in the text, because there's a future tense to this psalm. So what's better is not just that I shall not want in the *present*, but that I shall never want in the *future*. And if we translate this psalm in the future tense, it sounds something like this: *I shall never want. He will make me lie down in green pastures. He will lead me beside still waters. He will restore my soul. He will lead me in paths of righteousness for his name's sake,* and so forth. And when we see it in that way, we see this as the unfolding promises of God, his ongoing goodness toward his flock, that he provides everything both in the present and in the future, and that these promises extend all the way to forever.

In verse two, we're told, *he maketh me to lie down in green pastures, he leadeth me beside the still waters*. When it comes to sheep, something we need to know is that safety comes before rest. And so does food and so does refreshment. If a sheep is hungry or thirsty, or if it's upset about something, there is some danger, then he will not lie down and rest. So when it says that *he leadeth me beside still waters, he maketh me to lie down in green pastures*, that tells us that he creates a web of safety around us.

The *green pastures* obviously signify abundant provision, which is not a small deal when you consider that sheep are typically raised in arid climates where food can be difficult to find. This idea of *still waters* might better be understood as *waters of rest*, that it's not just a place to quench your thirst, but a place where you can have a satisfied restfulness.

This idea is expanded in a passage from Ezekiel chapter 34. And I'd like to share that with you. Listen to how Ezekiel 34—which by the way was written about 500 years after this psalm—how it echoes many of the ideas that we see today in Psalm 23. And I also want you to think in terms of how often you hear God say, *I will . . . I will . . . I will.* And what could be more certain than God saying, *I will?* So here it goes, Ezekiel 34.

> For thus says Lord Yahweh, "Behold, I Myself will seek My sheep and care for them. As a shepherd cares for his herd in the day when he is among his sheep which are spread out, so I will care for My sheep and will deliver them from all the places to which they were scattered on a cloudy and gloomy day. I will bring them out from the peoples and gather them from the countries and bring them to their own land; and I will shepherd them on the mountains of Israel, by the streams, and in all the inhabited places of the land. I will shepherd them in a good pasture, and their grazing ground will be on the mountain heights of Israel. There they will lie down on good grazing ground and be shepherded in rich pasture on the mountains of Israel. I will shepherd My flock, and I will make them lie down," declares Lord Yahweh. "I will search for the lost, bring back the scattered, bind up the broken, and strengthen the sick. . . ."

> "Then I will establish over them one shepherd, My servant David, and he will shepherd them; he will shepherd them himself and be their shepherd. And I, Yahweh, will be their God, and My servant David will be prince among them; I, Yahweh, have spoken."[47]

So 500 years or so between David writing this psalm and Ezekiel giving us this word from God. Now, who is this *David* that he's referring to? It can't be David, because David has been dead for hundreds of years by now. So there must be someone else—he's referring to someone who will be a son of David. And of course, that is Jesus Christ.

In verse three it says, *he restores my soul, he leadeth me in paths of righteousness for his name's sake*. We are in constant need of physical and spiritual restoration. I know I'm preaching to the choir because of the weakness of our body and because of the sin that clings so closely. And notice that sin has a way of driving us apart. It drives us away from the flock and it also drives us away from the Shepherd. So the Shepherd has to come and restore us.

How does he lead us? Well, he leads us by his Word and by his Spirit. So we should always strive to be exactly where he wants us to be at every moment, and especially to be content with that, whatever it happens to

[47] Eze 34:11-16a; 23-24 (LSB).

be. The Shepherd may lead us along difficult pathways, but he will never lead us into sin. Whenever we're tempted, he will always give us a way out. When it says that we *walk with the Lord* or *walk in his paths*, it means we walk according to his law. So we need to know what his law requires. There's always a path of righteousness in the midst of evil and in the midst of affliction. And we should remember that it matters how we respond to these things. Following the Shepherd means emulating his *pace* as well as staying in his *paths*—not getting ahead, not falling behind, not turning to the left, not turning to the right.

What is meant when it says that he does these things *for his name's sake*? It's referring to the honor and the glory of God. This is what it says in reference to his bringing his people out of bondage in Egypt. He said, *he saved them for the sake of his name*. Why? *That he might make his mighty power known*. God is always about the business of bringing glory to himself. And fallen men are always about the business of trying to steal God's glory.

Verse four:

> 4 Yea, though I walk through the valley of the shadow of death, I will fear no evil: for thou art with me; thy rod and thy staff they comfort me.

Here's realism. This is real life, because this life is going to be full of trouble. And it's precisely one of the reasons why we need a Shepherd to help guide us through this. Our suffering should be seen as an opportunity to draw closer to this Shepherd who meets all of our needs. In fact, I would say that it's wise to stay close to this Shepherd because you want to be close to him on the day when trouble comes. He promises to be with us in all of our troubles. He promises that nothing in this life or in the next life can separate us from him. And then it says, *I will fear no evil.* How can we be fearless? And the scripture says that *perfect love casts out fear*. That doesn't mean it removes the danger. We can have courage because God goes with us. Christ reminds us that *in this world we will have trouble, but take heart because I have overcome the world.*

Here's the remarkable charge that God gives to Joshua. This is right after Moses has died. Joshua is about to lead the people of Israel into the Promised Land. So in the first chapter of Joshua, God says this to him. Try to imagine him saying this to *you*—because through his word, he is speaking to you the same way.

> "Just as I have been with Moses, I will be with you; I will not fail you or forsake you. Be strong and courageous, for you shall cause this people to inherit the land which I swore to their fathers to give them. Only be strong and very courageous to be careful to do according to all the law which Moses My servant commanded you; do not turn aside from it to the right or to the

> left, so that you may be prosperous wherever you go. This book of the law shall not depart from your mouth, but you shall meditate on it day and night, so that you may be careful to do according to all that is written in it; for then you will make your way successful, and then you will be prosperous. Have I not commanded you? Be strong and courageous! Do not be in dread or be dismayed, for Yahweh your God is with you wherever you go."[48]

Joshua is on the verge of stepping onto the battlefield. The battlefield is a dangerous place, but God promises to be with him through that and to guide him through that using his law. We can't help but noticing that courage is one of the *commandments* of God to his people.

Those who are proud of heart have to be brought low before they can be brought closer to God. He guides us with his *staff*, and he disciplines us with his *rod*. Both of these are a comfort to us because they show the love of the shepherd for his sheep. The scripture tells us that *discipline is never pleasant in the moment that it happens, but it is the training that produces the peaceful fruit of righteousness*. We should keep in mind that he knows our needs better than we do. And he loves us too much to leave us in our sin. *Those whom he loves, he chastens*, and chastening brings us back into close fellowship with him and with each other.

[48] Josh 1:5b-9 (LSB).

Verse five says:

> 5 Thou preparest a table before me in the presence of mine enemies: thou anointest my head with oil; my cup runneth over.

The table that he prepares for us today is a shadow of the great feast that's awaiting us in heaven. The anointing oil that's referred to here is an expression of affection toward the guest of a banquet. It is also a picture for us of the Spirit whom God pours out upon us without measure. And this overflowing cup is the abundance of blessings that we receive each day. We could not count them all if we tried, especially starting with the cup of salvation. The misfortune is that we have so little sense of so great an overflowing of kindnesses and promises that God gives to us.

The New Testament tells us that Christ himself is the banquet. He says:

> "I am the living bread that came down from heaven; if anyone eats of this bread, he will live forever; and also the bread which I will give for the life of the world is My flesh."[49]

He also said:

---

[49] John 6:51 (LSB).

> "If anyone is thirsty, let him come to Me and drink." [50]

And:

> "Whoever drinks of the water that I will give him will never thirst—ever; but the water that I will give him will become in him a well of water springing up to eternal life."[51]

Christ is that fountain of eternal life. He's confounding his enemies when he refers to himself as *true food* and *true drink* in this passage from John 6. He says this:

> "Truly, truly, I say to you, unless you eat the flesh of the Son of Man and drink His blood, you have no life in yourselves. He who eats My flesh and drinks My blood has eternal life, and I will raise him up on the last day. For My flesh is true food, and My blood is true drink. He who eats My flesh and drinks My blood abides in Me, and I in him. As the living Father sent Me, and I live because of the Father, so he who eats Me, he also will live because of Me. This is the bread which came down out of heaven, not as the fathers ate and died. . . ."

Referring to the manna in the wilderness.

> "He who eats this bread will live forever."[52]

---

[50] John 7:37 (LSB).

[51] John 4:14 (LSB).

[52] John 6:53-58 (LSB).

By his own body and blood, he makes new life possible for all who believe.

This verse also refers to our enemies. He's setting the table *in the midst of our enemies*. And here's a couple of important points. Our enemies are *real* and they're also *present*. They're nearby. They may pose many dangers for us, up to and including death, but in the end, they will all be defeated. So we can have peace in the midst of our trials because we know God is in control and that he will bring good out of every kind of suffering.

At this point I'll ask, does he truly meet all of our needs? The first question we might ask is, *what about my sin?* And the answer is, *it's pardoned. There is therefore now no condemnation for those who are in Christ Jesus*. Then *what about my suffering?* He sanctified it. *For we know that all things work for the good of those who love God and are called according to his purpose*. Yes, but *what about death?* Death has been conquered. Death has lost its sting. *In all things we are more than conquerors. Nothing can separate us from the love of Christ. Our mortal bodies will give way to a body that lives forever*. Do we really understand the super abundance that we now possess? Or is it the case that we look so much at ourselves and the world around us that we miss what Christ has given to us? The problem is not with what we *have*, but whether we find *contentment* in what we have, and whether we look with *anticipation* to the life to come. If this God calls all of his stars by name, and if this God numbers all the hairs of your head, it's also the case that he calls all of his sheep by name as well. And then we can say with the apostle Peter:

> Therefore humble yourselves under the mighty hand of God, that He may exalt you at the proper time, CASTING ALL YOUR ANXIETY ON HIM, because He cares for you.[53]

What result do we get from all of these things?

> 6 Surely goodness and mercy shall follow me all the days of my life: and I will dwell in the house of the LORD for ever.

Well, that's not a bad conclusion. What does it mean for him to be my Shepherd? In short, it means that all of those promises are appropriated to me as an adopted son who is an heir in his Father's kingdom. F.B. Meyer calls goodness and mercy *the heavenly escorts who accompany us every day on our earthly pilgrimage.*

We shouldn't miss the fact that this last verse draws the line between this life and the next life. And death is the doorway from this life to the next. But we are carried through the veil of death to the Shepherd's doorstep to live in his house forever. This last verse is punctuated emphatically,

---

[53] 1 Pet 5:6-7 (LSB).

surely it says, with absolute certainty. So as this life passes day by day, we look forward to an unchanging eternity where we make our permanent home. The course of this life is merely a passage to the next. So follow your Shepherd closely and he will lead you home at last.

If you're not already a follower of this Shepherd, what do you need to do to be a follower of this Shepherd? Here's kind of a stunning thing that scripture tells us: that this good Shepherd didn't lay down his life to protect his sheep, he laid down his life so that the wolves who were his enemy could become his sheep. He gave his life for those who were determined to *kill* him in order that he could *save* them. Remarkable. We often forget that at one time we were all enemies of God. Perhaps some of you still are, and you need to settle that question today. Here's where the cry goes out, *be reconciled to God. Repent and believe the good news of salvation. Today is the day of your salvation*. Do not let it pass you by. How? The Shepherd is also the sheep gate. None enter except through him. No one else is qualified for this task. Don't look to anyone else for your salvation. Everyone else who claims to offer salvation for you is merely a hireling. They are not the true shepherds. There's only one pathway to God and it goes through his Lamb. So if you hear the voice of the Shepherd calling you today, through this word, make it your sole purpose to follow after him all the days of your life.

Jesus says this:

> "Truly, truly, I say to you, I am the door of the sheep. All who came before Me are thieves and robbers, but the sheep did not hear them. I am the door; if anyone enters through Me, he will be saved, and will go in and out and find pasture."[54]

Now this is a beautiful psalm, but it's not a psalm of sentiment. It's not designed just to make us feel good and give us a sense of hope that is just hanging in the air. The God who cares for his sheep had to give his own Son in order to purchase those sheep. And the same love that motivates his ultimate sacrifice also demands justice toward those who reject him. So do not leave yourself under the wrath of God, but come to him who offers the water of life freely to all who thirst for it. Put your trust in the one who keeps his sheep by the power of his promises—promises that can never fail.

F.B. Meyer summarizes this office of Shepherd in the following way:

> Christ has a shepherd's heart. He is full of love toward his sheep. He has a shepherd's eye that he oversees his whole flock. He has a shepherd's faithfulness, which will never forsake his flock. And he has a shepherd's strength to protect us from all evil and also a shepherd's tenderness, even to bear up the weakest on his own shoulders when we cannot stand on our own feet.

---

[54] John 10:7-9 (LSB).

I want to finish today with a short quotation by a biblical commentator named Thomas Scott. He says this:

> Let us thank him for the past and present, and trust him for the future: let us keep close to his service now; and simply repose our confidence in him, that his goodness will supply our every want, his mercy pardon all [of] our sins, and relieve all [of] our sorrows: that these shall follow us all the days of our life; and that we shall dwell in the house of the Lord forever; in his presence, where [there] is fullness of joy, and at his right hand, where [there] are pleasures forevermore.

Amen.

Let's pray. Father, we thank you for this beautiful word today. And I ask that you would apply it to each and everyone who's here and each who may be listening elsewhere—that they may be truly blessed, that they may come to know the Shepherd savingly, and that they will follow him all the days of their lives. In Christ's name we pray. Amen.

Exalted Over All (Psalm 46)

July 2, 2023

Our message today is Psalm 46, and I'll be reading from the *Legacy Standard Bible*. Hear the word of God.

1 God is our refuge and strength,
A very present help in trouble.
2 Therefore we will not fear, though the earth should change
And though the mountains shake into the heart of the sea;
3 Though its waters roar and foam,
Though the mountains quake at its lofty pride. Selah.

4 There is a river whose streams make glad the city of God,
The holy dwelling places of the Most High.
5 God is in the midst of her, she will not be shaken;
God will help her when morning dawns.
6 The nations roar, the kingdoms shake;
He gives His voice, the earth melts.
7 Yahweh of hosts is with us;
The God of Jacob is our stronghold. Selah.

8 Come, behold the works of Yahweh,
Who has appointed desolations in the earth.
9 He makes wars to cease to the end of the earth;
He breaks the bow and cuts up the spear;
He burns the chariots with fire.
10 "Cease striving and know that I am God;
I will be exalted among the nations, I will be exalted in the earth."

> 11 Yahweh of hosts is with us;
> The God of Jacob is our stronghold. Selah.[55]

The title of our message today is *Exalted Over All.* I think that may be the most important theme from this psalm. Easily enough, we think of it as being a comfort and assurance that God is a stronghold for us. But let's not miss that God deserves the glory for his power and his goodness.

I'll start by asking the question, *what is the worst trouble that you can imagine?* Got it in your mind? Now, what if God were to say something like this to you?

> Then God said to Noah, "The end of all flesh has come before Me; for the earth is filled with violence because of them; and behold, I am about to destroy them with the earth."[56]

Would you be a little concerned perhaps about your own welfare at this point—even if this declaration was immediately followed by instructions on how to build an ark?

Afterward, God says this:

---

[55] Ps 46 (LSB). Quoted again afterward.

[56] Gen 6:13 (LSB).

> "As for Me, behold I am bringing the flood of water upon the earth, to destroy all flesh in which is the breath of life, from under heaven; everything that is on the earth shall breathe its last."[57]

That's a very grim prognosis. It's foreshadowing or foretelling a calamity that's about to come in the days ahead. And at this point, you might be wondering whether that boat is going to be strong enough to get you through a storm like no other that's ever been seen. When we continue to read the text, however, what we see next is what we might call the *divine therefore*. The *divine therefore*, whenever God says *therefore*—in this case, *but*—there's usually some good news to follow.

> "But I will establish My covenant with you; and you shall enter the ark—you and your sons and your wife and your sons' wives with you."[58]

So yes, there's going to be a storm, but God is going to be with Noah and his family in the midst of the worst calamity that's ever come upon the face of the earth. So with those words of assurance, a promise from God—and his promises can never fail. Noah then does all that he's commanded and he is indeed saved from that flood along with all the creatures that went into the ark with him.

---

[57] Gen 6:17 (LSB).

[58] Gen 6:18 (LSB).

While there's no doubt that you have experienced danger and trouble in your life, I'm going to hazard a guess that you haven't encountered anything quite as severe as what Noah was faced with. And I'm using Noah's story to help us set the stage for Psalm 46, because it's a psalm that describes the very kinds of unthinkable calamities that Noah's family was not only told about, but they went through it. And then by that example, we can declare that *God is a very present help in trouble*. And what that means in this particular psalm is that his help has been well-proved from past experience. The simple lesson that we can take from the message today is that God who brings calamity on his enemies will also save his people from those same calamities.

I want to think of four things today as we work our way through this psalm. First of all, as odd as it may sound, God's *existence*. I'm going to start by talking about God's existence. And then we'll talk about God's *attributes*. And from there, we'll talk about God's *will*. And then we will talk about God's *work*. And that should make a nice way for us to understand the framework of Psalm 46.

A little background on this psalm. Many of the psalms that we've been looking at over these last few months are attributed to David. This one is not. It's called *A Song of the Sons of Korah*. And it's not from the time of David. It was probably from around 700 B.C. if we had to hazard a guess. It's 11 simple verses. There's also a *refrain* in this psalm. We have refrains in some of the songs that we sing in our time together here, so you know what that means—it's just a repetition of a certain idea that occurs at various points in the psalm. This psalm was beloved by Martin Luther and it's even referred to as *Luther's psalm*. And it was the inspiration for the hymn that he wrote called, *A Mighty Fortress Is Our God*. And I'll be making a couple of references to that during this message, and then we will sing it together at the end.

We could almost stop with the first and the last verses of this psalm. These two verses are worth remembering, and I'll repeat them a couple of different times. Here they are together, verse 1 and verse 11:

> 1 God is our refuge and strength,
> A very present help in trouble.
>
> 11 Yahweh of hosts is with us;
> The God of Jacob is our stronghold.

And I want you to notice the parallels between those two verses. Where in the first verse it says, *God is our refuge and strength*. In the last verse it says, *the God of Jacob is our stronghold*. The first verse, God is *a very present help in trouble*. And the last verse, *Yahweh of host is with us*. The rest of the psalm we might say, respectfully, is details, both in terms of the trouble we experience in this world, as well as the confidence that we have in the unshakable city of God. This world we know from experience is shaken again and again and again. Not so severely perhaps as in the days of Noah, but it's nevertheless in a state of turmoil. The other world that's referred to in this psalm cannot be shaken, and it cannot be shaken because God is in the midst of her, and God cannot be shaken.

Interestingly, our part in this affair, as we see in verse 10, is to just sit still, to be quiet, and watch and observe the work of God. While there is a time, of course, for us to strive in our Christian life—we think of the apostle Paul who says that he *strains toward the prize of the high calling in Christ Jesus*—there is also a time for us to stop and see and to remember the works of God. And that's what this psalm is about. In Luther's hymn, he says it this way: *were not the right man on our side, our striving would be losing*. Our fitting response, of course, to his desolations is to praise him for his deliverance.

Let's first think about God's *existence*. That seems like an obvious thing, but it's not so obvious in a day when so many try to deny the existence of God. The psalm starts with a statement of God's existence. God is stating the obvious, but these days it needs to be stated. And then within the refrain, *God is* shows up again. *Yahweh of hosts is with us. The God of Jacob is our stronghold*. We can't help but think of Genesis chapter one and verse one, where it says *in the beginning, God*. God was in the beginning of all things. Everything was created through him by his power and according to his will. I would put it like this, that God is what we might call the great precondition, meaning that he precedes all things and that all things depend upon him. And it somewhat goes without saying, but I'll say it anyway, that God has to *exist* before he can *act*. He must *be* in order to *do*.

A couple of verses that we could reinforce that with:

> By faith we understand that the worlds were prepared by the word of God, so that what is seen was not made out of things which are visible.[59]

And:

> All things came into being through Him, and apart from Him nothing came into being that has come into being.[60]

Fools will try to deny the existence of God. And when they do that, they prove their foolishness, don't they? Nothing can exist without him. And in fact, the Bible tells us that all men know in their hearts that there is a God. And this is why they work so hard to try to deny Him. They're trying

---

[59] Heb 11:3 (LSB).

[60] John 1:3 (LSB).

to deny the undeniable. The truth of God's existence, of course, is all around us in the things that he has made, including ourselves.

Several hundred years ago, there was a philosopher called Pascal who produced this idea called *Pascal's Wager*. The idea is that if we had to bet whether there was a God or not, we should probably bet that there is, rather than betting that there's not. Because if there is a God and we're wrong, we don't lose anything. But if we think there isn't a God and there is, then we have a significant loss. It's kind of a foolish argument.

First of all, we already know there's a God, and that the God who is there is the judge of all men. And unfortunately, Pascal's Wager doesn't really offer any remedy for that judge. I would add this, that simply believing in God puts you in the same category as demons, because they also believe in God and shudder. God's existence is irrefutable, because without him there would literally be nothing. The task for us then is first of all to know him *truly*, that is, as he reveals himself, and also to know him *savingly*, which means knowing him in his mercy and not knowing him in his *judgment*. And we'll see that only if God acts on our behalf, will we be able to say that *God is our refuge and our strength*. Otherwise, his power will be turned against us for the ultimate calamity. Noah's family was brought through the Flood according to the promise of God. Everyone else perished because of their wickedness. That Flood continually reminds us that God will indeed make a distinction between the righteous and the unrighteous.

Let's consider some of God's *attributes*. Think about how often in the Bible God reveals something about himself by his names. And there are several different names that God uses in this short psalm. First of all, *God*; also *Yahweh*; then also *the God of Jacob*; and *Yahweh of hosts*. And we shouldn't miss as well, he uses the expression *Most High*. So we have all of those names that are revealed to us in this psalm that give us some idea of his person, his character, his purposes. There are two that I'm going to look at, the two that appear in the refrain. What does the refrain say?

> Yahweh of hosts is with us;
> The God of Jacob is our stronghold.

Let's look at those two names and think about how that reveals something about God. There's an interesting contrast between these two names because one refers to his relationship with heavenly creatures, the angels, and the other refers to his relationship with someone who was a very earthly creature, that is, Jacob.

Yahweh of hosts. What does that mean? We often hear that. And I think the translation is typically a little unhelpful because the way that we use *host* is not necessarily the way the translators are using the word *host*. It's from a Hebrew word called *Sebiot* from which we get the English word, *Sabaoth*. So in Luther's hymn in a little while, we will see it says, *Lord Sabaoth his name*. What does *Sabaoth* mean? It means pretty loosely, a mass of people who are organized for war, an army. We have this idea that this Lord Yahweh is commander of an army. And we don't need a lot of imagination to see that this commander is the Lord Jesus Christ. We'll look at a few verses here that point that out to us.

I want to start in the book of Joshua in chapter five. Joshua is on his way to Jericho for the first of what will be many military conquests in the Promised Land. And what happens on the road? He runs into someone unexpectedly. This is what the scripture says:

> Now it happened when Joshua was by Jericho, that he lifted up his eyes and looked, and behold, a man was standing opposite him with his sword drawn in his hand, and Joshua went to him and said to him, "Are you for us or for our adversaries?"
>
> He said, "No! Rather I indeed come now as commander of the host of Yahweh." And Joshua fell on his face to the earth and bowed down and said to him, "What has my lord to say to his slave?" The commander of the host of Yahweh said to Joshua, "Remove your sandals from your feet, for the place where you are standing is holy." And Joshua did so.[61]

---

[61] Josh 5:13-15 (LSB).

This Commander was obviously God. And the way that we know that is because Joshua worshiped him.

In the Garden of Gethsemane, very different scenario. Garden of Gethsemane, Jesus says that he has legions of angels that are at his command. Here's what the text says from Matthew 26:

> Then they came and laid hands on Jesus and seized Him.
>
> And behold, one of those who were with Jesus stretched out his hand and drew out his sword and struck the slave of the high priest and cut off his ear. Then Jesus said to him, "Put your sword back into its place; for all those who take up the sword shall perish by the sword. Or do you think that I cannot appeal to My Father, and He will at once put at My disposal more than twelve legions of angels? Therefore, how will the Scriptures be fulfilled, which say that it must happen this way?"[62]

A legion at that time could be as many as 6,000 soldiers. So 12 legions—*more* than 12 legions—means more than 70,000. And we might wonder what 70,000 angels could do to any army of mere men.

Much later in the New Testament, we read something very interesting because it takes us back to a time before the Flood. The little book of Jude says this, referring to Enoch:

---

[62] Matt 26:50b-54 (LSB).

> But Enoch, in the seventh generation from Adam, also prophesied about these men, saying, "Behold, the Lord came with many thousands of His holy ones, to execute judgment upon all, and to convict all the ungodly of all their ungodly deeds which they have done in an ungodly way, and of all the harsh things which ungodly sinners have spoken against Him."[63]

This passage comes at the very end, almost the very end of the New Testament, and it goes back to a period almost a thousand years before the Flood. So there was a message, a warning of judgment, even in the very early days before Noah.

I'll share this last example with you from the book of Revelation, and near the end of the book, Revelation 19. John in his vision says:

> Then I saw heaven opened, and behold, a white horse, and He who sits on it *is* called Faithful and True, and in righteousness He judges and wages war.
>
> His eyes are a flame of fire, and on His head are many diadems; having a name written on Him which no one knows except Himself, and being clothed with a garment dipped in blood, His name is also called The Word of God. And the armies which are in heaven, clothed in fine linen, white and clean, were following Him on white horses. And from His mouth comes a sharp sword, so that with it He may STRIKE DOWN THE NATIONS, and He will RULE THEM WITH A ROD OF IRON; and HE TREADS THE WINE PRESS OF THE

[63] Jude 14-15 (LSB).

> WRATH OF THE RAGE OF GOD, the Almighty. And He has on His garment and on His thigh a name written, "KING OF KINGS, AND LORD OF LORDS."[64]

This one who commands the armies of God is no less than Jesus himself. The imagery of these kinds of passages ought to be enough to terrify us because no man will stand against this great warrior King in the day of his wrath. But there is good news.

There's good news for the sinner because this *Yahweh of hosts* is also *the God of Jacob*. He is the savior of men. And here's the comfort. If you know something about the life of Jacob, you know that hardly anyone in the book of Genesis needed to be saved more than Jacob. His name, in fact, means *cheater*. And he spent most of his life involved in one kind of swindle or another, cheating and being cheated. It's frankly scandalous that God identifies himself with a man whose name stands for rebellion. Nevertheless, God promises to be with him and to bless him, to apply to him the same covenant promises and blessings that were given to his father Isaac and to his grandfather Abraham.

The following examples will demonstrate God's grace towards Jacob. The first scenario is that after he steals the blessing from his brother Esau, he becomes a fugitive. His mother says, *you better get out of here. Go to Haran.*

---

[64] Rev 19:11-16 (LSB).

Your brother's angry. He wants to kill you. So he starts his journey and this occurs:

> And he reached a certain place and spent the night there because the sun had set; and he took one of the stones of the place and put it under his head and lay down in that place. Then he had a dream, and behold, a ladder stood on the earth with its top touching heaven; and behold, the angels of God were ascending and descending on it. And behold, Yahweh stood above it and said, "I am Yahweh, the God of your father Abraham and the God of Isaac; the land on which you lie, I will give it to you and to your seed. And your seed will also be like the dust of the earth, and you will spread out to the west and to the east and to the north and to the south; and in you and in your seed all the families of the earth shall be blessed. Behold, I am with you and will keep you wherever you go. And I will bring you back to this land; for I will not forsake you until I have done what I have promised you."[65]

Jacob spends the next twenty years in exile, working for his uncle Laban, who was also a cheater. And after those twenty years, God speaks to him and says, *it's time to go home*:

> Then the angel of God said to me in the dream, 'Jacob,' and I said, 'Here I am.' He said, 'Lift up now your eyes and see that all the male goats which are mating are striped, speckled, and mottled; for I have seen all that Laban has been doing to you. I am the God of Bethel, where you anointed a pillar, where you

[65] Gen 28:11-15 (LSB).

> made a vow to Me; now arise, leave this land, and return to the land of your kin.'"[66]

And the journey back home was quite an adventure because on the way he encountered an encampment of God's angels. It's very interesting that this is mentioned so briefly and casually as if it's an everyday thing. It says:

> Now Jacob went on his way, and the angels of God met him.
>
> Then Jacob said when he saw them, "This is God's camp." So he named that place Mahanaim.[67]

That name means *two camps*, referring to his and to the angels'. Then a very short time later, he has another encounter, this time with God, who appears to him and they wrestle all night long. And it's on this occasion that Jacob is renamed *Israel* because he has grappled with both men and God. The text says this:

> Then Jacob was left alone, and a man wrestled with him until the breaking of dawn. And he saw that he had not prevailed against him, so he touched the socket of his thigh; and so the socket of Jacob's thigh was dislocated while he wrestled with him. Then he said, "Let me go, for the dawn is breaking." But he said, "I will not let you go unless you bless me." So he said to

---

[66] Gen 31:11-13 (LSB).

[67] Gen 32:1-2 (LSB).

> him, "What is your name?" And he said, "Jacob." Then He said, "Your name shall no longer be Jacob, but Israel; for you have striven with God and with men and have prevailed." Then Jacob asked him and said, "Please tell me your name." But he said, "Why is it that you ask my name?" And he blessed him there.[68]

We see that God is *Jacob's* God, and the encouragement for us is that he can be *our* God as well. He was not Jacob's God because Jacob was a paragon of virtue. We know that as far from the truth. But in spite of Jacob's moral failures, he receives these promises of God. Meanwhile, his brother Esau does not receive those promises. We need to understand that Jacob didn't receive the promises because he was better than Esau, but because God was gracious to him.

Now, very interesting, at the end of Jacob's life, he's essentially on his death bed, and he is speaking a word about all of his sons at this point in his life before he dies. And he has this to say regarding his son Judah:

> "The scepter shall not depart from Judah,
> Nor the ruler's staff from between his feet,
> Until Shiloh comes,
> And to him shall be the obedience of the peoples."[69]

---

[68] Gen 32:24-29 (LSB).

[69] Gen 49:10 (LSB).

While that sounds very enigmatic, basically what it means is that there is going to be a *ruler*, one who has a *scepter*, who is going to prevail, who is going to be a *king* to whom the obedience of the nations will be given. And of course, that's referring to the Messiah who will come almost 2,000 years later.

Now a ruler who is a thousand years after this will also be promised a king from his family line, and that's King David. And so this Messiah, when he comes, will be called both the *son of Abraham* and the *son of David.* And it's this Son who will be the basis on which sinners can be reconciled to God, to be brought from a relationship of enmity into a relationship of peace.

Let's consider God's will. This is fairly simple, actually. There's not a whole lot to say about this because it's given to us very clearly in verse 10, the second part of verse 10, where it says:

> "I will be exalted among the nations. I will be exalted in the earth."

So we see that God's will is to be exalted. And we have this repetition in verse 10. And whenever we see repetition, we need to be thinking that this must be important if it's been said more than once.

In verse four, he's also called *Most High*. That's a title that's used elsewhere. *Elyon*. This name gives us another important insight into his nature, because God dwells in a high and holy place. And *holy* has a couple of meanings. One is the meaning of purity, perfection, spotlessness, but it also refers to a separation, someone who is set apart.

The apostle Paul describes him in this way, referring to God, as:

> He who is the blessed and only Sovereign, the King of kings and Lord of lords, who alone has immortality and dwells in unapproachable light, whom no man has seen or can see. To Him be honor and eternal might! Amen.[70]

God reminds us elsewhere that he shares his glory with no one:

> "I am Yahweh, that is My name;
> I will not give My glory to another,
> Nor My praise to graven images."[71]

The psalmist in Psalm 115, we notice, refuses to take credit for God. Listen:

> Not to us, O Yahweh, not to us,
> But to Your name give glory

---

[70] 1 Tim 6:15-16 (LSB).

[71] Is 42:8 (LSB).

> Because of Your lovingkindness, because of Your truth.
> Why should the nations say,
> "Where, now, is their God?"
> But our God is in the heavens;
> He does whatever He pleases.[72]

How is God exalted then? He alone deserves all glory because of his being and his majesty. He brings glory to himself, both in the display of his love and mercy, as well as in the display of his justice.

We also know that he is near to the brokenhearted. The prophet Isaiah says this:

> For thus says the One high and lifted up
> Who dwells forever, whose name is Holy,
> "I dwell on a high and holy place,
> And also with the crushed and lowly of spirit
> In order to revive the spirit of the lowly
> And to revive the heart of the crushed."[73]

Those who are oppressed by the guilt of their sin can find relief by placing themselves on the mercy of God, for he will abundantly pardon.

---

[72] Ps 115:1-3 (LSB).

[73] Is 57:15 (LSB).

Let's now take some time to think about God's works. He works in these two ways, both *for* his people and *against* his enemies. Now this word *desolations* is an interesting word because it literally means *astonishments*. Things that we would say, *you'd have to see it to believe it*. And even if you see it, you might not believe it. It's that unbelievable. We might say it's the kind of things that only God can do. And it's one of the reasons why I started with the example of Noah's Flood, because this was not a natural event. This was a work that God brought upon the earth.

Some scholars will say that this psalm is referring to the destruction of Sennacherib's army during the days of Hezekiah. And you'll recall that the angel of Yahweh killed in one night, 185,000 soldiers of the Assyrian army. That is certainly an impressive desolation. Now, the language of this psalm actually reminds us of miracles of deliverance from Egypt. So we're going to take some time to think about that. So after the ten plagues and before crossing the Red Sea, we find, not surprisingly, the Israelites are already forgetting God's works. And yes, they're starting to complain.

The scripture says this:

> Now Pharaoh drew near, and the sons of Israel lifted up their eyes, and behold, the Egyptians were marching after them, and they became very afraid; so the sons of Israel cried out to Yahweh. Then they said to Moses, "Is it because there were no graves in Egypt that you have taken us away to die in the

> wilderness? What is this you have done against us in bringing us out of Egypt? Is this not the word that we spoke to you in Egypt, saying, 'Leave us alone that we may serve the Egyptians'? For it would have been better for us to serve the Egyptians than for us to die in the wilderness." But Moses said to the people, "Do not fear! Stand by and see the salvation of Yahweh which He will accomplish for you today; for the Egyptians whom you have seen today, you will never see them again forever. Yahweh will fight for you, and you will keep silent."[74]

This is the one who brings the plagues of destruction upon Egypt—the one who parts the Red Sea, the one who delivers his people to safety, and the one who destroys the army of the enemy.

There are passages in some of the psalms that provide a summary or a recollection of past events. And one of those is found in Psalm 78. And I would like to read about 15 verses from Psalm 78 that pertain to this, and listen at how God is using this to remind his people of his works. He says:

> 40 How often they rebelled against Him in the wilderness
> And grieved Him in the wasteland!
> 41 Again and again they tested God,
> And pained the Holy One of Israel.
> 42 They did not remember His power,
> The day when He redeemed them from the adversary,
> 43 When He performed His signs in Egypt

[74] Ex 14:10-14 (LSB).

And His miracles in the field of Zoan,
44 And turned their rivers to blood,
And their streams, they could not drink.
45 He sent among them swarms of flies which devoured them,
And frogs which destroyed them.
46 He gave also their crops to the grasshopper
And the fruit of their labor to the locust.
47 He killed their vines with hailstones
And their sycamore trees with frost.
48 He gave over their cattle also to the hailstones
And their herds to bolts of lightning.
49 He sent upon them His burning anger,
Fury and indignation and distress,
A band of destroying angels.
50 He leveled a path for His anger;
He did not hold back their soul from death,
But gave over their life to the plague,
51 So He struck all the firstborn in Egypt,
The first of their vigor in the tents of Ham.
52 But He led forth His own people like sheep
And guided them in the wilderness like a flock;
53 He led them safely, so that they did not fear;
But the sea covered their enemies.

54 So He brought them to His holy land,
To this hill country which His right hand had acquired.
55 He also drove out the nations before them
And apportioned them for an inheritance by measurement,
And made the tribes of Israel dwell in their tents.[75]

[75] Ps 78:40-55 (LSB).

A recollection of what God did in bringing Israel out of Egypt and judging the Egyptians. But how quickly we forget that God is gracious in showing that these psalms, and indeed the whole scriptures, the historical narratives of scripture, are given to us in part so that we will what? So that we will *remember* his great work. In spite of the desolations against Egypt, his people Israel almost immediately forgot. And of course, when they forgot, they were afraid. And when they were afraid, they started to complain. Don't we do the same thing? We have to be told to *remember* because we so easily forget God and his works.

Now, interestingly in Psalm 78 verse 41, the *New King James Version* renders it like this, that *they limited the Holy One of Israel*. And that strikes me as interesting because it's as if we're saying he can't do what he says he wants to do. And here again, we do the same kind of thing, but we're told that he is able to do *exceedingly abundantly more than we ask or think*. The reason we don't *have*, scripture tells us, is because we don't ask in *faith*, believing that he will do it, or that we ask according to our own desires so that we waste the gifts that he would give to us.

We see that it is God who brings desolations. He is the one who does the *shaking*, to use the language of this psalm. But he himself cannot be shaken, nor can his heavenly home be shaken. He who calls the worlds into existence also calls the nation *dust on the scales*. And as we saw in

Psalm 2 a little while back, he laughs from heaven whenever the nations conspire to overthrow his rule. This one who *makes wars to cease* makes peace because he wins the battle. Will the one who melts the earth with the sound of his voice have any difficulty overcoming his enemies and protecting his children? I should think not. Can any man stand in his own strength against the one who can move mountains? Absolutely not.

Your circumstances are certainly not as severe as the earth coming apart at the seams. If God can help in the most extreme circumstances, he can certainly help in all lesser troubles. For us, we should not be like stubborn Israel who so easily forgets.

As we prepare to close, let's think for a few minutes on God's call to all mankind. This is going out to all the nations, all the earth. Verse 10:

> "I will be exalted among the nations. I will be exalted in the earth."

Is not the voice of God also Christ? The word of God. Is not Christ the Commander of the Lord's armies? Is he not *Mahanaim*, the second camp that surrounded Jacob? And does he not promise to come with ten thousands of his holy ones? Are you of like faith with Abraham who looked forward to a city built by God? Are you even now living with him by the Spirit while you remain on this short pilgrimage?

We have to be aware not to become attached to the things of this world, which we're told are all passing away. Else when God shakes this world, as he will in the last judgment, we will be shaken along with it, and all will be lost. We must hold everything loosely and remember that we are to take nothing with us. In Luther's hymn, he says it this way, *let goods and kindred go, this mortal life also*. How will you be reckoned among God's army and not among his enemies? You will either conquer *with* him or you will be conquered *by* him. He is the King of Kings and Lord of Lords, but he is also the Lamb of God who takes away the sin of the world. How is your sin taken away? By turning away from your sin and putting your trust in Christ. Here's what may be the most astonishing work of God: that the one who commands the armies of heaven is also the God who saves a sinner like Jacob. In other words, cheaters like us who deserve nothing but judgment.

How are we to know God and know his way of salvation? Not only by his works, but by his words. The Bible should be precious to us because it contains everything God needs to tell us. Martin Luther says this about it:

> No matter what happens, you should say, there is God's word. This is my rock and anchor. On it I rely and it remains. Where it remains, I too remain. Where it goes, I too go.

This world is under judgment and will be judged on the last day. The promise of God is to protect his people in the same way he protected Noah during the most destructive storm of judgment this world has ever seen.

What does this psalm tell us? First, that *we will not fear*. Also that *we will stand still* to behold the works of God and that *we will exalt and worship the Most High*. We will seek our salvation in the one who is our refuge and our strength.

> God is our refuge and strength, a very present help in trouble . . . . Yahweh of hosts is with us. The God of Jacob is our stronghold.

Let's pray. Father, we ask that you would apply these words to us today. Ensure that each and every one who hears is indeed one of your adopted children. I pray that you would bring salvation where it's necessary, that you would strengthen our faith, that you would be with us and show yourself to be with us through all the trials of this life, that we may look forward to that heavenly city where there's a river that brings glory to you, and that river is Christ himself. In his name we pray. Amen.

Man's Darkness and God's Light (Psalm 36)

August 20, 2023

Today we'll be considering Psalm 36. And today I've chosen the *English Standard Version* (ESV) for this psalm. Twelve verses.

Hear the word of the Lord:

1 Transgression speaks to the wicked
deep in his heart;
there is no fear of God
before his eyes.
2 For he flatters himself in his own eyes
that his iniquity cannot be found out and hated.
3 The words of his mouth are trouble and deceit;
he has ceased to act wisely and do good.
4 He plots trouble while on his bed;
he sets himself in a way that is not good;
he does not reject evil.

5 Your steadfast love, O LORD, extends to the heavens,
your faithfulness to the clouds.
6 Your righteousness is like the mountains of God;
your judgments are like the great deep;
man and beast you save, O LORD.

7 How precious is your steadfast love, O God!
The children of mankind take refuge in the shadow of your wings.
8 They feast on the abundance of your house,
and you give them drink from the river of your delights.

9 For with you is the fountain of life;
in your light do we see light.

10 Oh, continue your steadfast love to those who know you,
and your righteousness to the upright of heart!
11 Let not the foot of arrogance come upon me,
nor the hand of the wicked drive me away.
12 There the evildoers lie fallen;
they are thrust down, unable to rise.[76]

As we look at this psalm today, I want to think about how, if you were to ask the average person on the street, and maybe even the average person in the church, whether he's going to heaven or not, what kind of an answer you would get. And for the most part, you're going to get a favorable response. And then if you were to ask a follow-up question, why, naturally, would a person have such confidence in his own salvation? He's almost as likely to answer that it's because he has tried to live a good life, or he might say that he's done more good than bad during his life. If you were to ask as well a more general question, whether he thinks mankind as a whole is basically good or basically bad, he would almost certainly tell you that he thinks man is basically good. The irony is that this is fallen man trying to assess his own condition. And we might say in this case that fallen man, when he's asked to judge himself, gives himself a very light sentence. He would say, *no one's going to try to argue that man is perfect. We all make mistakes. To err is human.* We use those

[76] Ps 36 (ESV). Quoted again afterward.

kinds of expressions to express the idea that it's unreasonable to expect that man could ever be perfect. Of course not. So why then, in the light of that obvious admission, do we continue to insist on our own inherent goodness? And then we have to ask, what about those that we know that are really, really, really bad? How do we explain the very worst of the behavior that we see around us?

We might notice a pattern that modern man, when asked to explain his behavior, typically will explain it in terms of blaming someone else. We might even notice that the blame game started back in the Garden of Eden. And he does this as if none of his choices actually reflect the desires and intentions of his own heart. In fact, this is an older expression that I'm sure all of you will recognize. It's not as common today, but back in the old days, we used to say *the devil made me do it*—as if we are under the direct control of the devil himself. Now, if you listen to man try to defend himself like this, you might wonder whether he ever took any responsibility for any of his own moral choices or the consequences of his moral choices. We could argue that it's a consistent pattern of behavior that whenever man does whatever he does, he's always going to try to justify himself in it no matter how destructive it may be. And he's always going to come up with some good reason for it. So we go back to the original question: is man basically good or bad? What does the Bible have to say in answer to that question? And the answer it turns out is so offensive that we really try to find every way we can to get out of it. And that includes the opening verses of this psalm that we're considering today.

There was a song years ago called *Bad to the Bone*. Maybe some of you remember that. Man is not just *bad to the bone*, to use that expression. It's actually much worse than that. That evil goes to the very thoughts and desires of the heart. In fact, we remember Jesus saying that *it's not what goes into a man that makes him unclean, it's what comes out of him that makes him unclean*—that evil comes from the inside. Now, if this verdict seems too harsh, I might remind you at this point that God destroyed the whole world with a flood because of the wickedness of fallen man. And I want to quote a couple of verses from Genesis 6 just to remind you. Here's what the verdict was that God pronounced against the world at that time:

> The LORD saw that the wickedness of man was great in the earth, and that every intention of the thoughts of his heart was only evil continually.[77]

And then the proof is in the pudding, so to speak, verses 11 and 12, where it says:

[77] Gen 6:5 (ESV).

> Now the earth was corrupt in God's sight, and the earth was filled with violence. And God saw the earth, and behold, it was corrupt, for all flesh had corrupted their way on the earth.[78]

We could argue at this point that in those days, the whole world was begging for judgment. And in fact, judgment came in the way of the Flood. Now, when we turn to Psalm 36, we see an uncomfortable glimpse into just that same kind of ugliness of man's sin. And the interesting thing about this psalm in terms of how it's put together is that it's contrasted to the shocking goodness of God in those middle verses. The transition, in fact, from verse four to verse five is so abrupt that there are some scholars who suppose that this can't be a single psalm, that it must be more than one psalm that was put together by an editor. But if it is indeed inspired by God to be written just this way, then the contrast that we see here is going to serve to demonstrate the lovingkindness of God towards those who have earned nothing but judgment. The contrast here finds its analogy in the starkness between dark and light. So we must be prepared, first of all, to see the darkest of the dark in the heart of fallen man before we then see the brightness of the glory of God in the middle verses. We can think of it something like sitting in a room that's pitch black and then suddenly the blinds are pulled and the light of day, the light of the sun comes beaming through the window. And it's virtually blinding to us because our eyes have adapted to the dark. So we see that

[78] Gen 6:11-12 (ESV).

contrast in this psalm between the darkness of man's sinful heart and the beauty of God's moral perfections.

I'm going to consider this psalm today in the three divisions that it falls into, *man's moral corruption*, which is where we'll spend most of our attention today. Then the middle section is *God's boundless mercy*. And the third section is a petition at the end of the psalm that expresses *the believer's confidence*.

Just a little background to set the stage. It's a psalm that's attributed to David. Many of the psalms that we've looked at in our studies have come from the pen of David. David lived about 3,000 years ago. So we have an idea of how long this psalm has been in our possession. The specific occasion for it is unclear. So the date of writing is not clear as well. And the catch with this psalm, this is kind of the technical part of our discussion today, is that the opening verse is a little difficult to translate because it's not entirely clear in that very first part of verse one, who's *speaking* and who's *listening*. So if you're reading a different translation than the one that I'm using today, it might read a little differently. I've chosen the ESV today, the *English Standard Version*, because it seems to provide a consistent flow of thought from that first verse through the rest of those opening verses.

First we'll consider in those first four verses, *man's total corruption*. I'll reread those first four verses:

1 Transgression speaks to the wicked
deep in his heart;
there is no fear of God
before his eyes.
2 For he flatters himself in his own eyes
that his iniquity cannot be found out and hated.
3 The words of his mouth are trouble and deceit;
he has ceased to act wisely and do good.
4 He plots trouble while on his bed;
he sets himself in a way that is not good;
he does not reject evil.

This is by no means the only psalm in the Bible that speaks about the intrinsic evil of fallen man. In fact, we're going to see how this part of this psalm is used in the New Testament and how it's combined with several other passages, mostly from the psalms, to make the argument about the universal guilt of man. In Psalm 14, for example, we read that *the fool says in his heart, there is no God*. You're familiar with that one. And it's almost as if in his foolishness, he thinks that by simply saying there is no God, he can make God somehow disappear. And in this psalm, we see another facet of that same foolish person, that he has no fear of God, that God will not find out his sin and judge him for it.

Doesn't this sound a lot like the judgment of God against the world in the days of Noah? At this point, we could ask, do we think that the nature of mankind has changed since before the Flood? And the answer is *no*. Is this not what we see both in past history as well as in the unfolding history of the present moment? We looked at Psalm 2 some time ago and it opens with that question, *why do the nations rage and the peoples plot a vain thing*? You see mankind raging against God and against Jesus and trying to throw off all rule from heaven as if they could do such a thing. So it's a pattern since the Fall that man is trying to remove himself from the authority of God.

In the introduction, we saw the problem of the man on the street who claims to believe in God, attempting to justify himself. *I've basically been a good person*, that kind of thing. But let's not miss the point. If he does say something like that, he's thinking of himself as righteous in his own eyes and not righteous according to God's standard. In fact, when he says that God is going to judge him favorably for his efforts, he's not thinking of the God of the Bible at all. He's actually imagining a God who does not exist. So he can try to say that he believes in God and yet still have no fear of God. It's not necessarily the case that the one who has no fear of God says there is no God, but he often does. For such a one, it's the knowledge and the fear of the *true* God that has been extinguished in his heart and in his mind. And it's extinguished by the very evil nature that he's trying to deny. Although he cannot escape the God of the Bible, he does everything he can to remove himself from God's influence by setting himself intentionally against God in his thoughts, in his words, and in his deeds.

Notice again the verdict. God who examines the heart sees only wickedness in the heart of man, no matter how deep he goes. Man's own assessment of himself is that he might be bad, but there's some nugget of righteousness deep down. Yet the word of God makes it clear that the deeper you go into the recesses of the man's heart, the worse it gets. One of the Puritans once referred to the heart as *a fountain of impurity*. There's nothing but evil that can come from it. Man always tries to defend himself with the claim that underneath all of that wickedness, there must be some good. We just have to look closely enough in order to find it. It's also the case that because God is patient, again, we can think of the days of Noah. God is patient in withholding his judgment. And we'll see this in the next part of the psalm. And the wicked man wrongly thinks that God doesn't see his sin and that will not bring him into judgment. And indeed, there are other psalms in the Bible where we find the psalmist expressing his bitter lamentation that the wicked sometimes seem to prosper more than the righteous. How do we explain the affliction of the righteous, for example? Has God forgotten them? Is God angry with them? Has he cast them off? Have the wicked prevailed over the righteous? No, not at all. What we see is that God is longsuffering even toward the wicked because he intends to show mercy to many of them. And as for the affliction of the righteous, God promises to use it for their good.

I think almost reactively about the story of Jacob's son, Joseph, who was hated by his own brothers. He was sold into slavery and was sent down to Egypt. His brothers never thought they would ever see him again. And yet what happened? In God's purposes, he was sold into slavery and became the prime minister of Egypt. And from that position of authority, when the famine came, he was able to save his whole family. And then after the death of Jacob, a very interesting thing happened. His brothers said, *uh-oh, dad's gone. Joseph's going to come after us for what we've done*. So they confront him and say, *dad told us to let you know not to do anything to us after he died*.

Joseph's response is classic:

> But Joseph said to them, "Do not fear, for am I in the place of God? As for you, you meant evil against me, but God meant it for good, to bring it about that many people should be kept alive, as they are today. So do not fear; I will provide for you and your little ones." Thus he comforted them and spoke kindly to them.[79]

---

[79] Gen 50:19-21 (ESV).

Joseph could have taken revenge against his brothers, but he understood that God—working even through the evil purposes of his brothers—meant to bring about their salvation.

As we see in this psalm, the wicked man always judges himself righteous, because in reality, he's only comparing himself to himself. That's an easy way to pass the test, isn't it? He's not comparing himself to God. He lives according to the lie of his heart. And that could mean that he thinks there's no God at all, or he might think that there's a God who will judge him just as favorably as he judges himself—even being willing to attribute good intentions to his egregious moral failures. We could sum up the wickedness of the wicked by noticing that he's characterized by a proud heart—one who opposes God at every opportunity and yet he counts his rebellion as if it were a virtue. He thinks that he's sufficient in himself. He doesn't have any remorse for his evil deeds because his heart is simply incapable of remorse, either the offense that he has toward God or the offense and the hatred of his fellow man. We could put it like this, that pride—going back to the original fall when Satan rebelled against God—that pride is the *first* and the *worst* sin that separates us from God, and the proud cannot be reconciled to him.

If the wicked man is able to set aside the fear of God, guess what? There's now no restraint to hold him back from his sin. Whatever he can devise in his imagination, he's now going to seek the opportunity to carry it out. Sin is his constant meditation. It preoccupies his thoughts and it does that because it reflects the deepest desires of his hard heart. His twofold evil is in the failure to do good and in the pursuit of wickedness. He neglects the one and he pursues the other. He is so far from virtue that nothing good can be expected to come from him.

Once a man is freed from all the restraints of his evil desires, he's going to seek to stamp out any opposition that attempts to hold him accountable, so anything or anyone that reminds him of the Bible's God must be violently opposed. And by this we understand that persecution often comes against God's people by the wicked. The wicked man is motivated by a deep-seated hatred of God and of man. And that explains his insatiable violence toward the weak. In his selfish ambition, he sees people simply as a thing to be used and discarded, not a thing to be loved and protected. We understand—and we have seen through the ages—that for the wicked man, life has no value. Where does this kind of pure evil come from? How do we explain something like this? It's manifested first in the spiritual realm. That's where it begins. Satan and his demons who rebelled against God and who now do all that they can during the time that they have to draw men into their wicked schemes. If they could, they would destroy God. But because they can't destroy God, they resort to every kind of evil and every kind of violence they can devise against

God and against everything in his creation. Satan himself is even called at one point by Jesus, *the father of lies*. And in the book of Revelation, he's referred to as *the destroyer*. Destruction is what marks his rebellion.

In this psalm, we should see verse one as a warning of just how deep and pervasive wickedness is in the man who does not fear God. He will become a terror to society, especially if he makes his way into a position of authority. And we'll look at the psalm next month, Psalm 94, where in verse 20, it warns us that wicked rulers make wicked laws. It says *they frame injustice by statute*. They make it law and then use unjust laws against righteous people. Here, Psalm 36 makes it clear that no matter how far you go down into a wicked man's heart, there is no shred of goodness there. There is nothing to commend him in his own eyes or in God's eyes. All his darkness and sin, right down to his innermost desires and thoughts. It's the very opposite of what men think of themselves. And such an ungodly man can only go from bad to worse in his own strength. He can't improve himself. It shouldn't take us by surprise when we see wicked men, the scripture says, *going from bad to worse*, but our frequent surprise shows that we still don't understand just how bad man's condition is. Even the worst of us want to attribute some good to mankind.

If we want to understand the full impact of these verses here, we need to notice how the apostle Paul uses *there is no fear of God before his eyes* as a capstone for his argument in the book of Romans that *all* men of *all* kinds are *all* under the judgment of sin. This is what he says:

> What then? Are we Jews any better off? No, not at all. For we have already charged that all, both Jews and Greeks, are under sin, as it is written . . .

What he's going to say next is quotation from the Old Testament:

> "None is righteous, no, not one;
> no one understands;
> no one seeks for God.
> All have turned aside; together they have become worthless;
> no one does good,
> not even one."
> "Their throat is an open grave;
> they use their tongues to deceive."
> "The venom of asps is under their lips."
> "Their mouth is full of curses and bitterness."
> "Their feet are swift to shed blood;
> in their paths are ruin and misery,
> and the way of peace they have not known."

And here it is:

> "There is no fear of God before their eyes."

He goes on to say this:

> Now we know that whatever the law says it speaks to those who are under the law, so that every mouth may be stopped, and the whole world may be held accountable to God. For by works of the law no human being will be justified in his sight, since through the law comes knowledge of sin.[80]

In other words, it's the law that we think we can keep that actually exposes the fact that we can't keep it and that we need to be rescued from the power of sin.

In this passage in Romans 3, Paul is making his point here by quoting from Psalm 5, Psalm 10, Psalm 14, Psalm 36 (that we're looking at here), Psalm 140, and also the 59th chapter of Isaiah. All of those are quotations are from the Old Testament. In other words, when we see this description of the wicked man and his evil motivations, we have to understand that scripture is talking about every one of us. No one escapes this judgment. Paul is pronouncing this judgment against the whole world. Even the *best* of us—I would put it this way—has the potential to be the *worst* of us. And if you haven't reflected on that a little bit, you might want to consider that—just how bad you have the potential to be apart from the grace of Christ.

---

[80] Rom 3:9-20 (ESV)

So in this state of mankind, he is completely lost in sin, and he does not have the power to save himself. He cannot save himself by his obedience to the law, to good works. There was an opportunity to be saved by works, but that was a long time past. That was when God first made Adam and Eve and made them perfect. And they disobeyed and brought the curse upon the whole world. So now in man's condition, after the Fall, the only thing that can possibly save him is *the tender mercy of God*. And that is what we see in these next verses. Listen:

> 5 Your steadfast love, O LORD, extends to the heavens,
> your faithfulness to the clouds.
> 6 Your righteousness is like the mountains of God;
> your judgments are like the great deep;
> man and beast you save, O LORD.
>
> 7 How precious is your steadfast love, O God!
> The children of mankind take refuge in the shadow of your wings.
> 8 They feast on the abundance of your house,
> and you give them drink from the river of your delights.
> 9 For with you is the fountain of life;
> in your light do we see light.

One commentator tries to express these verses as follows. He says, *in these verses, all that is infinite, sublime and unfathomable in nature is made emblematic of the perfections of Jehovah*. The best of what we can imagine in this created world gives us just a glimpse of the wideness and the beauty of God's mercy.

There is *one* God, but we're starting to see as this psalm transitions, that he's relating to *two* different kinds of men. There is one stream of mankind that's called *wicked*, and another stream of mankind that is called *righteous*. In our studies of the psalms, we have often seen this contrast between the wicked and the righteous. The question now is, what is the difference between them? And the difference is how God relates to them. To the wicked, he shows himself to be *just*, and to the righteous, he shows himself to be *merciful*. That division began way back in the Garden when God told the Serpent, *I will put enmity between your seed and her seed*. That division and that conflict remain in the present age. It's an irreconcilable conflict between good and evil, light and dark, God and Satan. We notice that man has become part of that war with God, against God by his willful rebellion. He is sided with the Serpent.

In this portion of the psalm, there's an implied contrast between the wicked and the righteous. The implied contrast is that the righteous *do* fear God. They have come to understand that he is a God of justice who executes judgment against the wicked. Now here's the light of God's goodness. Here the light of God's goodness breaks in against the black backdrop of man's evil heart. The contrast is quite striking. But we come to this point, and now we have to demand an answer to an important question. What is it that separates the wicked from the righteous? What is it that makes an evil man come to the place of fearing God? The answer is found in a little Hebrew word called *hesed*. It's usually translated *lovingkindness*. And here we have the tender mercy of God. And this tender mercy of God has the power to transform his enemies into his adopted children. The man who fears God has received that mercy. He now understands his own evil nature and the wrath that his sin deserves. And that by his own power, he was not able to lay hold of this lovingkindness of God. It was given to him as a gift. And with that gift, he placed himself onto the mercy of God, who now takes away his sin and reconciles him to himself. The one who has received this tender mercy has received a new nature contrary to the old nature—a new nature that now hates sin and loves God. And listen to how many different ways the Bible describes this. *Behold, the old has gone and the new has come*. God says that he will *remove the wicked man's dead heart of stone and replace it with a living heart of flesh* or that *the dry dead bones of the old nature can be made to live again by the power of the word of God*. That *the man who was dead in sins and trespasses, God has now made alive in Christ*. That this man *was born again into a new and living hope*. That *he was born again, not by the will of man, but by the will of God*. And those kinds of descriptions go on in both the Old Testament and the New Testament. We see that *what was impossible for man*—saving himself by the law—*is possible for God*, that he can be saved by grace. Though *the leopard cannot change his spots, though the Ethiopian cannot change the color of his skin*, God can change the nature of the fallen man and restore it again to its original perfection. That the one who was God's enemy can be reconciled to him and brought into a relationship of peace, *putting to death the enmity*, *nailing our record of sins to the cross* where they are paid in full by the Son of God.

We have to understand that God's mercy is not something that man *earns*, and it's not something that he *deserves*. It is that favorable lovingkindness of God to those who deserve only judgment. That's *hesed.* In the New Testament, it's *grace*. The *fear* of God produces a *love* for God. Those who take refuge in him find that he meets their needs abundantly. Think of the description here of having all the riches of God available to his children. He is never stingy towards those upon whom he sets his gracious lovingkindness—and just as a tender father who has mercy on his children and withholds none of his riches from them.

Next, I want to look at one part of a certain verse here, where it says, *in your light, we see light*. It almost sounds as if David is speaking in circular language here. Is he doing that? Is he saying something that we can't unravel? Or is it the case that when he describes a *light* that allows us to see *light*, that he's using this to mean two different things? Consider it this way. The *first* light is revealing something about the *second* light. Here's where the apostle John helps us out. At the beginning of his gospel, he says, *in him*, referring to Christ, *was the light of life and the life was the light of men*—and he connects both the *light* and the *life* in the person of

Christ. He goes on to say that *the glory of God reveals the glory of the Son*, so that the light of God became the light of the world in the person of Jesus Christ. And Jesus can then tell his disciples that if they have seen him, they have also seen the Father. Christ is that same light that also searches the hearts of men to reveal what is there in those deepest recesses. There is no corner of the heart that the light of God does not expose. So that brings us back to the first few verses of this psalm. One of our commentators says it this way, *that Divine light, which shines in the scripture, and especially in the face of Christ, the Light of the world has all truth in it.*[81] So we have the contrast between light and dark, between truth and lies. And it's that truth of God that we see in these middle verses that makes the diagnosis we see at the beginning of this psalm possible. The judgment against man is severe precisely because the goodness of God is absolutely perfect.

Notice how this verdict in Psalm 36:1, which Paul quotes in Romans chapter three, suddenly gives way. This is what Paul says right after that passage that I quoted you.

> For there is no distinction: for all have sinned and fall short of the glory of God, and are justified by his grace as a gift, through the redemption that is in Christ Jesus, whom God put forward as a propitiation by his blood, to be received by faith. This was

[81] Matthew Henry and Thomas Scott.

> to show God's righteousness, because in his divine forbearance he had passed over former sins. It was to show his righteousness at the present time, so that he might be just and the justifier of the one who has faith in Jesus.[82]

So just as all men have *sinned*, all men are offered this free gift of *grace*. It's being offered to you at this very moment, if you would have it. And by laying hold of it, you receive that tender mercy of God and the abundance of his lovingkindnesses towards all those who receive Christ by faith.

The last three verses of this psalm are a short *petition* where David says:

> 10 Oh, continue your steadfast love to those who know you,
> and your righteousness to the upright of heart!
> 11 Let not the foot of arrogance come upon me,
> nor the hand of the wicked drive me away.
> 12 There the evildoers lie fallen;
> they are thrust down, unable to rise.

Here is the short petition for a continuation of God's lovingkindness and for protection from the wicked. God knows the wickedness of the wicked and he also knows how to protect his own people from them. God promises to catch the wicked in his own snares. This present contrast between the wicked heart in verse one and the upright heart in verse ten

[82] Rom 3:22b-26 (ESV).

could hardly be more striking. The knowledge of God is accompanied by the righteousness of God that cleanses the sinful heart from all sin and guilt and shame. The future contrast between the wicked reaches its climax at the end of this psalm. That climax is at the judgment: for the righteous, eternal blessedness, fellowship, and abundance of every good thing. For the wicked, everlasting destruction by *the worm that does not die* and by *the fire that cannot be quenched.* Here's the warning: that those who refuse to know God in his lovingkindness and who refuse to seek refuge under his wings will soon come to know God in the terror of his judgment. There will be no remedy for God's wrath on the day of judgment when man will be judged in righteousness according to every thought, word, and deed. God is indeed the one who marks iniquity. He keeps meticulous records in heaven, and at the judgment the books of the records of sin will be opened to reveal everything. But for the redeemed, the redeemed has faith in the promises of God and that is sufficient to bear him up under the trials of this life.

I want to close with a short quote from one of the commentators who pulls these ideas together very nicely for us today. He says:

> Faith calls things that are not as though they were. It carries us forward to the end of time. It shows us the Lord sitting on his throne of judgment, the righteous caught up to meet him in the

> air, the world in flames under his feet, the empire of sin fallen to rise no more.[83]

Let's pray. Father, it is a fearful thing to fall into the hands of the living God. I pray that you would make the minds and the hearts of men wise to know you, to know your righteousness, and to know that you have provided a way for any man to be reconciled to you in this life through the person and the work of Jesus. I pray that you would, by your Spirit, make these words effectual in the hearts of all who hear them. In Christ's name we pray. Amen.

---

[83] Matthew Henry and Thomas Scott.

The Judgment of the Unjust Ruler (Psalm 94)

September 17, 2023

Psalm 94 from the *Legacy Standard Bible*.

1 O Yahweh, God of vengeance,
God of vengeance, shine forth!
2 Be lifted up, O Judge of the earth,
Render recompense to the proud.
3 How long shall the wicked, O Yahweh,
How long shall the wicked exult?
4 They pour forth words, they speak arrogantly;
All workers of iniquity vaunt themselves.
5 They crush Your people, O Yahweh,
And afflict Your inheritance.
6 They slay the widow and the sojourner
And murder the orphans.
7 They have said, "Yah does not see,
Nor does the God of Jacob discern."

8 Discern, you senseless among the people;
And when will you have insight, you fools?
9 He who planted the ear, does He not hear?
He who formed the eye, does He not see?
10 He who disciplines the nations, will He not rebuke,
Even He who teaches man knowledge?
11 Yahweh knows the thoughts of man,
That they are vanity.

12 Blessed is the man whom You discipline, O Yah,
And whom You teach out of Your law;
13 That You may grant him calm from the days of calamity,
Until a pit is dug for the wicked.

14 For Yahweh will not abandon His people,
Nor will He forsake His inheritance.
15 For judgment will again be righteous,
And all the upright in heart will follow it.
16 Who will arise for me against evildoers?
Who will take his stand for me against workers of iniquity?

17 If Yahweh had not been my help,
My soul would soon have dwelt in the abode of silence.
18 If I should say, "My foot has stumbled,"
Your lovingkindness, O Yahweh, will hold me up.
19 When my anxious thoughts multiply within me,
Your consolations delight my soul.
20 Can a throne of destruction be allied with You,
One which forms trouble by statute?
21 They band themselves together against the life of the righteous
And condemn the innocent to death.
22 But Yahweh has been my stronghold,
And my God the rock of my refuge.
23 He has brought back their iniquity upon them
And will destroy them in their evil;
Yahweh our God will destroy them.[84]

In our recent studies, including last time when we looked at Psalm 36, we've talked a lot about the contrast between the righteous and the wicked. This is a contrast that keeps showing up over and over again in the psalms—this very stark contrast. Remember the opening verse from Psalm 36 that we considered last time when it said, *transgression speaks to*

[84] Ps 94 (LSB). Quoted again afterward.

the heart of the wicked deep in his heart. There is no fear of God before his eyes. And then we spent time looking at what that means. What does that look like? How does a man behave when he has no fear of God? And the answer is that he behaves quite wickedly. This time around, the psalmist is expressing his desire to see God exercise judgment against wicked rulers—specifically those who will use their position of power to afflict those who are defenseless. So that is the contrast that we see in this psalm. Those who are doing the afflicting, which are those who are in power—and those weak and defenseless who suffer under their affliction, even to the point of death. This is a message we can relate to. We certainly live in a time when people who are in power are using and abusing their authority in ways that enrich themselves and take advantage of those who are less fortunate.

As we look at this psalm, we're seeing at the very opening a call for vengeance, but we need to understand that this is not a repudiation of authority. It's not that there is something wrong with authority *per se*, but it's a reminder that those who are in authority have a duty to love and to serve those who are in their care. Think of how parents are required to take care of their children. It's similar to that idea. And anyone who abuses that authority is going to face the judgment of a righteous God for failing in those solemn responsibilities. So this psalm is a warning for anyone in a position of authority, whether it might be in the home or in the church, in the workplace, or in this case, it's specific to those who are in power, the power of government. In the meantime, this psalm, interestingly, is also a psalm of encouragement for those who suffer under that kind of affliction, that God is going to give comfort to them in their affliction. And there is the promise that he will deliver them from the hand of the wicked in due time.

Today, I want to consider this psalm in its four natural divisions. First, we see the psalm open with *a cry for justice* from the God of justice. Secondly, there is a call by the psalmist for those who are defying God to *get wisdom*, to be wise. Thirdly, we see an expression of the *confidence* that the psalmist has in the midst of his affliction that God will comfort him and deliver him. And lastly, *the certainty of judgment* for the wicked and for the deliverance of those who are oppressed. So it falls into those four natural divisions. We'll take a look at each in turn.

A little background first. We think of the psalms typically as being *prayers*, and as we've seen, not all of them are prayers, but this one certainly is. It begins as a cry to God and it ends the same way. There is also during the course of this psalm, a change in voice, which is to say that there are others who are being addressed in the midst of this psalm, including those rulers who were oppressing the righteous. We don't know who the author of this psalm is. Scholars believe that it's one of the later psalms, which would put it well past the time of David and Solomon, probably about 2,500 years ago. So again, as we look at some of these writings that are 2,500 or 3,000 years old, and we hear how they're speaking, they sound like they're talking about what's happening today. And it's a reminder that there's really *nothing new under the sun*, as Solomon says—there's nothing new about those in authority oppressing the weak and the defenseless.

Next I'll make a comment about literary structure. I know it's a little odd. It seems kind of out of place to mention that, but if you read this psalm, and I encourage you to read it after we are done here today, something you notice in the way that it's written, typical of Hebrew poetry, is that it has lots of *parallelisms*. In other words, lots of *repetition*. It seems like the psalmist is saying the same thing over and over again, and he is, and the point of that is to emphasize or bring attention or boldness to those points. We also see that this psalm incorporates a number of *questions*. He's throwing questions in there as a way of getting our attention and bringing out his points. This psalm follows what is a common theme in the psalms, which is *affliction and deliverance*. So we see both affliction and deliverance unfolding in the text here. There's also some instruction and some warning. It's a reminder to those who are rulers that they are accountable to the one who is the judge of all the earth. And then we can say that it's both a *general* and a *specific* warning. It's a general warning to anybody in any position of authority, but it's a very specific warning to those who hold positions of power.

So now let's look at this psalm in its four parts. Firstly, what we will call *the cry for justice* in these opening seven verses. Let me reread that for you. And listen for the parallelism that I just mentioned.

> 1 O Yahweh, God of vengeance,
> God of vengeance, shine forth!
> 2 Be lifted up, O Judge of the earth,
> Render recompense to the proud.
> 3 How long shall the wicked, O Yahweh,
> How long shall the wicked exult?
> 4 They pour forth words, they speak arrogantly;
> All workers of iniquity vaunt themselves.
> 5 They crush Your people, O Yahweh,
> And afflict Your inheritance.
> 6 They slay the widow and the sojourner
> And murder the orphans.
> 7 They have said, "Yah does not see,
> Nor does the God of Jacob discern."

These opening verses are a prayer to God from the afflicted. Now it was nothing unusual for Israel to be afflicted by her enemies on the outside, but something unique about this situation in Psalm 94 is that the affliction seems to be coming from the inside. It is Israel, the rulers of Israel, afflicting their own people, brother against brother. Now in our previous studies, we were considering how bad man is in his fallenness.

And in this psalm today, we can begin to see how much affliction the wicked man can do when he is in a position of power and authority. So we'll say that this psalm is not a call for vigilante justice, but it's a cry for God to intervene on behalf of the afflicted. And as we think about how God is being described in this psalm, how he's being named, he's being named in his various attributes. He's not just a God of *vengeance*, but he's a *holy* God. And a holy God is going to vindicate his name. He is not going to permit his creatures to rebel against him forever. In this psalm, the call is for him to shine forth his justice against the evildoers who are afflicting and murdering the weak—showing himself in his righteousness and vindicating his glory and his holiness by his judgment.

God can and will judge because he is the king over all the earth and all earthly rulers. When they defy justice, they should understand they're placing themselves under the judgment of God. Now, how did the wicked get power over the weak? Well, that's a story we're familiar with. We see that happening all the time in all kinds of ways. But often that's going to happen by an assortment of *lies* and *false promises*. Does that sound familiar? I think that's the definition of politics, isn't it? And that once they're in power, they have a tendency to abuse their authority in order to hang on to their authority. And in fact, they will even turn against their own people in doing that. Something we see in these opening verses that should jump out at us is that something that marks the wicked is their pride and their arrogance. They're proud and they're boastful. So in their speech and in their deeds, they exalt themselves.

Spurgeon has this to say:

> It's the nature of workers of iniquity to boast, just as it is a characteristic of good men to be humble.

Here we encounter a question in these opening verses, *how long . . . how long?* It's a common question. And merely asking the question suggests that the one who's afflicted is near to the breaking point if he does not get an answer, if God does not respond. Part of what we should see in this lamentation is that it's a demonstration that God is longsuffering even toward the wicked. He does not destroy them at once. But the wicked should not believe because God delays his judgment that God doesn't know what they're up to, or doesn't care about their evil deeds. In other words, his longsuffering is neither a case of indifference on his part, and it is certainly not a case of his giving approval to wrongdoing. Here we could look at some words from Solomon when he says in the book of Ecclesiastes chapter eight verses 11 through 13:

> Because the sentence against an evil work is not executed quickly, therefore the hearts of the sons of men among them are given fully to do evil. Although a sinner does evil a hundred times and may prolong his life, still I know that it will be well for

> those who fear God, who fear Him openly. But it will not be well for the wicked man, and he will not prolong his days like a shadow, because he does not fear God openly.[85]

God is patient and longsuffering towards wickedness. And we'll see in the psalm just a little later, how God uses that affliction in the life of the righteous.

Who's doing this affliction? Again, it's God's own people who are turning against themselves. This represents, if anything, an aggravated sin for God's people to be afflicted by his own people. It's a very high-handed kind of rebellion for the Israelites to treat each other in an abusive way. It's not just what we would call *perverted* justice, but *inverted* justice. In other words, these are rulers who turn justice upside down. The defenseless are destroyed, and at the same time, those who are doing wickedness are excused for their deeds.

What does oppression look like? We get a little bit of a picture from this psalm. We would say that it's not merely a deprivation of freedom, but it's *harm* toward those to whom *justice* is due. The psalmist is calling on God now to defend the defenseless when it seems at this point that all other defenses have failed, all other avenues have been exhausted. Now, oppression is what you get when you have power without love. And

---

[85] Ecc 8:11-13 (LSB).

again, think of what it's like to be a parent. A parent is to be authoritative toward his children, but in love and not in an abusive or an unkind way. The problem, of course, is that men in their sin love the exercise of power more than they love their fellow men. And so you end up with some of the worst forms of abuse. It's not unusual for a tyrant to look for ways to limit the strength of his opposition. We think of what Pharaoh did to the Israelites when they were in captivity in Egypt. And on two different times in two different ways, he ordered a form of genocide against the Israelites in order to do what? To limit their numbers and to limit their strength.

Those who are most easily oppressed include four different categories. Three are mentioned in this passage, and I've added the fourth one just to round out the picture. Widows, orphans, foreigners, and those who are poor. And what is the common element? These are people who do not have a *protector*. A widow does not have a *husband*. An orphan does not have a *father*. A foreigner does not have the rights of a *citizen*. And those who are poor simply may not have the resources or the standing to defend themselves.

There are a number of names and titles of God that are included in this psalm and I'll mention them here. *Yah*, we have seen *Yahweh*, *God*, *the God of vengeance* as the psalm opens, and then *the God of Jacob*, *the judge of the earth*, and toward the end of the psalm, he's also called a *stronghold* and *a rock of refuge*. Familiar terms that we apply to God. And the significance of terms like *Yahweh* and *God of Israel*, or *God of Jacob*, I should say, is that that is expressing the covenant relationship that God has with his people. It's a very special, particular, intimate kind of relationship. It is a familiarity, which makes this kind of sin even more unjustifiable.

In the next four verses, we have *a call to wisdom*. Listen to what the psalmist says to the unrighteous:

> 8 Discern, you senseless among the people;
> And when will you have insight, you fools?
> 9 He who planted the ear, does He not hear?
> He who formed the eye, does He not see?
> 10 He who disciplines the nations, will He not rebuke,
> Even He who teaches man knowledge?
> 11 Yahweh knows the thoughts of man,
> That they are vanity.

We'd have to say that this is a pretty brazen exhortation that the psalmist is making to his oppressors. He's calling them *fools* and *senseless*, and why? It's because they think God can't see what they're up to, that he doesn't *hear*, he doesn't *see*. The one who formed the eyes and the ears somehow does not have sight or hearing himself. Now, at this point, we could ask, what is the point of trying to reason with the wicked if they are really senseless fools? And I think the answer is that they may, like the prodigal son—we can think of him—they may come to their senses. There is still a reason, a motivation for warning the wicked about their wickedness and encouraging them or exhorting them to turn from their wickedness.

God not only sees and hears, but guess what? He also knows the very thoughts and the motives of the man. In other words, it's not just what he's seeing from the outside, he knows what's on the inside. And you might remember how we talked about that last time, even that opening line in Psalm 36, how *wickedness speaks to the man deep in his heart*. It goes all the way down to the bottom. God knows all of the thoughts and the motivations of the wicked man. This has to be true. This has to be true or otherwise, if God did not know the heart, then he could not truly be the judge of the world. So God has to have comprehensive knowledge in order to be a just judge.

In verse 11, The psalmist calls man's thoughts *vain*. This is the same word that Solomon uses over and over again in the book of Ecclesiastes. *Vanity of vanities, all is vanity*. And what that means quite literally is that it's *vapor*. It's something that's *transient*. It doesn't last. It's here one moment and gone the next. The idea that's captured by that is *futility*—because anything that passes away obviously is not stable. It's not something you want to try to hang anything on.

The catalog of wicked deeds in these opening verses, including murder, point to an ingrained wickedness in this evil ruler. There's this pride of insolence in oppressing the weak, and at the same time foolishly believing that God does not see or hear when in fact God knows his very thoughts. And if this is the God who disciplines the nations, that is, the *pagan* nations, then certainly he can discipline his own people as well. He disciplines the nations in part to protect his own people from those nations. But he also has the power to discipline those who are rulers of his own people. And the warning here is that no nation should ever think that it's outside of God's reach, or exempt from God's judgment. And frankly, that's a message that we need to hear in our country today. We should not think that our wickedness has gone unnoticed by God.

The commentator H.C. Leupold says this, that *God is in the habit of disciplining the nations by the course of history*. In other words, not to get too far down a rabbit trail, but as you read the Old Testament histories, what you see is nation fighting against nation, always nation against nation. And it's that course of history that's being referred to here. Nation against nation has the effect of disciplining and subduing evil rulers. Psalm 68 refers to God as a father of the fatherless, and a judge for the widows. So where there is no human protector, God stands in that place of protection over those who are oppressed. Proverbs 23 warns us about this:

> Do not move the ancient boundary. . . .

Stones used to be used back in those days as boundaries between property.

> Do not move the ancient boundary
> And do not come into the fields of the orphans,
> For their Redeemer is strong;
> He will plead their case against you.[86]

In other words, don't try to steal from somebody because you think they are easy to steal from. God will defend them.

Part of what we see in this psalm is that oppressors will try to shield themselves from earthly accountability. But in the end, their office is not going to protect them from divine accountability. Because as we are told, *to whom much is given, much is required*. And those who occupy positions of leadership, we can say, *will be judged more strictly*. Now in the meantime, even when all other power has been taken away from the weak, they still have the power to *speak*. And the truth is one of the most powerful things that we can use in order to preserve justice and to speak against the unrighteous.

---

[86] Prov 23:10-11 (LSB).

Next, thirdly, we want to consider *the confidence that the psalmist has in his affliction*. It's not to minimize the severity of the affliction, but it's going to turn the tables somewhat. It's going to give us a different way to think about this affliction from the standpoint of the one who's being afflicted. So listen to these verses:

12 Blessed is the man whom You discipline, O Yah,
And whom You teach out of Your law;
13 That You may grant him calm from the days of calamity,
Until a pit is dug for the wicked.
14 For Yahweh will not abandon His people,
Nor will He forsake His inheritance.
15 For judgment will again be righteous,
And all the upright in heart will follow it.
16 Who will arise for me against evildoers?
Who will take his stand for me against workers of iniquity?

17 If Yahweh had not been my help,
My soul would soon have dwelt in the abode of silence.
18 If I should say, "My foot has stumbled,"
Your lovingkindness, O Yahweh, will hold me up.
19 When my anxious thoughts multiply within me,
Your consolations delight my soul.

You see the change in the mood in this psalm suddenly, that it doesn't diminish the affliction, but it puts a different spin on it by looking at it from the standpoint of how God can use it to actually bless the righteous. So the psalmist is now redirecting his prayer back to God in this part of the psalm. It's a striking change in tone. There's a consolation here both because the psalmist is remembering his past deliverance and he also is expressing an expectation of deliverance from the present affliction. And how often in our lives can we look back, especially over the years, and see how God has delivered us from an assortment of afflictions? And the one who has delivered us *will* deliver us.

The question is posed twice, *who . . . who?* Who's going to come to my rescue? And of course the answer is *Yahweh.* And what a rescuer he is. And here's the opposite of the futility of the thoughts of the wicked. The confidence in the God of eternity. God does not change. The thoughts of the wicked man will come and go. They will be gone in a moment, but the God of eternity will be forever.

How does the law of God teach man? And the answer is often by his disobedience. And disobedience leads to discipline. Discipline leads to correction, and correction then leads to greater obedience. Even the most faithful believer still needs discipline because he is not yet fully conformed to the image of his perfect Savior. What is the danger that the psalmist is referring to here when he says that he might stumble? Well, we can look at a similar lament in Psalm 73 in verse three, where he says, *for I was envious of the boastful. I saw the peace of the wicked*. And is it not a temptation for those who are in affliction to begin to envy the ones who are afflicting them when they see their prosperity? What then is going to hold up the afflicted when he's about to stumble? It's going to be God's tender mercy. Remember, we've talked about that in the past, that word *lovingkindness* shows up over and over again. *Your lovingkindness, O Yahweh, will hold me up*. What is that? That is the tender mercy of God, what we call *grace* in the New Testament. We see that the affliction of the righteous is used for their good. God can turn the affliction of the righteous into good. It's a form of discipline and correction and training for those who are righteous, and for the wicked who are carrying out those evil deeds it will be for their destruction in the day of judgment.

Just as we said that God's forbearance of evil is not his approval, neither should we think if we're the ones being afflicted, that it's an abandonment of his people. He has not abandoned us. We have to be careful. And the warning in this psalm for us as believers is not to judge entirely by outward appearances because by outward appearances, it looks like the wicked are prospering and the righteous are suffering. So the word of God allows us to see the bigger picture when the wicked flourish—and even when the righteous perish. We know that it's for the good of those who are called of God and that it will be for judgment of those who do not repent.

William Graham Scroggie says this:

> Afflictions should lead the righteous man to rest and patiently wait until the day of retribution comes, as it assuredly will.

So that is our confidence even in the midst of affliction.

Now lastly, *the certainty of judgment*, the last four verses.

> 20 Can a throne of destruction be allied with You,
> One which forms trouble by statute?

In other words, *the wicked ruler makes wicked laws*. Verse 21:

> 21 They band themselves together against the life of the righteous
> And condemn the innocent to death.
> 22 But Yahweh has been my stronghold,
> And my God the rock of my refuge.
> 23 He has brought back their iniquity upon them
> And will destroy them in their evil;
> Yahweh our God will destroy them.

This last section begins with another question and it's going to conclude very abruptly with the certainty of God's righteous judgment against the wicked.

We see, perhaps a little more clearly in this part of the psalm, his assurance is coming from personal experience. And notice how the tone of the psalm changes where he starts referring to God as *my* stronghold and *my* refuge. Very personal terms. As we said earlier, the power of an office is designed by God for the care and the protection of the weak. And it's an abuse of that office when rulers fail to do that. Those men are predators who then abuse the power of the office to afflict the powerless in order to advantage themselves. And that's inevitably what's at the bottom of it, isn't it? It's not just the desire to push down one, but to elevate oneself.

The one who is a civil magistrate or a civil ruler is perhaps the one who can do the most damage because he has the widest authority over a nation or over a land. He has the authority to make his own law. And not only that, but he also has the power of the sword, which is the power to take life. Now that power is designed to be used against the evildoer, but the evil ruler is going to use that power against the righteous. There's often a connection as well between the one who is guilty of oppression and injustice, and one who takes bribes. We see that in many other places in scripture, even though it's not mentioned in this particular psalm. The one who takes bribes to do *what?* To pervert justice, to exonerate the guilty and to afflict the innocent.

Proverbs 29, verse four, says this:

> By justice the king causes the land to stand,
> But a man of bribes tears it down.[87]

In chapter 10 of Isaiah, the first two verses, he says this:

> Woe to those who enact evil statutes
> And to those who constantly record mischief,
> So as to turn the poor away from their cause
> And rob the afflicted of My people of their justice,
> So that widows may be their spoil
> And that they may plunder the orphans.[88]

Scroggie says this:

> God is not the ally of those who sin in high places and who do wrong under the shelter of legal forms, who rush upon the righteous and condemn the innocent.

But when you have the power to make law, you have at least some power to try to protect yourself from your own evil designs, from the consequences. Authority also makes it possible to expand and to consolidate power. How many tyrants are content with a small tyranny? They want to expand the boundaries into other areas. And another thing that we see in verse 21 here is a wicked *collaboration*—wicked rulers

---

[87] Prov 29:4 (LSB).

[88] Is 10:1-2 (LSB).

surrounding themselves with wicked *confederates*. And as we look at scripture more broadly, we see how princes and judges and prophets and priests, in times of wickedness and abuse, will band together in their evil deeds. I would put it like this: it should be no surprise when a corrupt *church* allies itself with corrupt *rulers*. And I think we are living in that kind of a time.

Besides framing unjust laws, rulers can exercise other forms of abuse. We see these things almost on a daily basis. One is just ignoring the law. The law is there, but they just ignore it. Or the law is there, and they say, *this is what it says, but this is what I want it to mean*. And they just reinterpret it. Another is to enforce the law selectively against one, but not against another. Wicked rulers do not respect the limits of their offices. They will always try to take authority from other lawful jurisdictions, such as the church or such as the family, or in some cases, maybe whole countries invading their neighbors and taking over other countries. For certain, those whose throne is corrupt have made themselves enemies of God.

Just when we're ready to lose heart—I know you want a little encouragement here—just as we're ready to lose heart, we encounter what I consider quite possibly the two most important words in the Bible—*but Yahweh. But Yahweh*. Because those two words change everything. God acts above all earthly powers of evil, and he brings good out of it all. He is a stronghold for the righteous, and he is a judge of the wicked. The psalmist's confidence is expressed in the language of mutual ownership. And again, I would encourage you to reread this psalm and meditate on this point. We are *his* people and *his* inheritance, and he is *our* God.

God's anger is always constrained by his righteousness. God is never out of control when he carries out vengeance. In other words, God never avenges more than what justice requires. Unlike us, when we want vengeance, we usually want to get back more than what is owed.

Do God's own people escape judgment when they abuse their authority? Do they think they will receive a lighter sentence? Certainly not. Paul reminds us in 2 Corinthians 5:

> For we must all appear before the judgment seat of Christ, so that each one may be recompensed for his deeds in the body, according to what he has done, whether good or bad.[89]

And Spurgeon says this about unjust rulers:

> God enters no alliance with unjust authority, he gives no sanction to unrighteous legislation. . . . They legalize robbery

[89] 1 Cor 5:10 (LSB).

> and violence, and then plead that it is the law of the land; and so indeed it may be, but it is a wickedness for all that.

As we bring our message to a conclusion today, let's think about a few points. Part of the lesson from this psalm is that it's appropriate for the people of God to turn to him in times of oppression. God can and will deal with the wicked according to their deeds. At the same time, we should remember that vengeance belongs to God alone. In other words, we are free from the law of vengeance. We trust God to account for all sin and either he will forgive the sinner in Christ or the sinner will repay for all of his wicked deeds under God's justice. And that frees us to be able to love and to forgive our enemies, even in the midst of persecution. Again, God's justice is the *exact* repayment of what a man's sin deserves. It's a kind of justice that we cannot attain in this life. Vengeance is also a vindication of God's name—that it is *his* character that is ultimately at stake when men do their evil deeds.

Here we need to remember that we were once enemies of God in need of his mercy. And that having received that mercy, we now seek to turn others away from sin and toward righteousness. That second stanza of the psalm, that warning to the wicked, is an example of how we bring the wicked to a knowledge of their sin and then by God's grace, have an opportunity to lead them to salvation in Christ. In the midst of our afflictions, we shouldn't lose heart. We should continue to praise the name of him who rules from heaven and the one who promises to set all wrongs right when he returns in glory. In the meantime, we can bear up under affliction just as children under the discipline of a righteous father and we can look to him for consolation in all of our present trials.

I would like to let Spurgeon have the last word in this sermon today. He says this:

> The natural result of oppression is the destruction of the despot; his own iniquities crush him ere long. Providence arranges retaliations as remarkable as they are just. High crimes in the end bring on heavy judgments, to sweep away evil men from off the face of the earth; yea, God himself interposes in a special manner, and cuts short the career of tyrants while they are in the very midst of their crimes.

Let's pray. Father, thank you for the word that you've given to us today. And I pray for the encouragement of all the afflicted, not only here, but around the world, that they may take heart knowing that affliction is but for a moment, that deliverance will come, that justice will reign in the end. Help us each in our various situations to continually look to you for the consolation that we find in Christ our Savior. In his name we pray. Amen.

The Prince Who Reigns Forever (Psalm 146)

October 15, 2023

Our scripture for today is the 146th Psalm. If you have a Bible, you can turn to the very back of the Psalter and find it very quickly that way. It's a fairly short psalm, 10 verses, and it goes like this. I'll be reading today from the *Legacy Standard Bible* (LSB).

1 Praise Yah!
Praise Yahweh, O my soul!
2 I will praise Yahweh throughout my life;
I will sing praises to my God while I have my being.
3 Do not trust in nobles,
In merely a son of man, in whom there is no salvation.
4 His spirit departs, he returns to the earth;
In that very day his plans perish.
5 How blessed is he whose help is the God of Jacob,
Whose hope is in Yahweh his God,
6 Who made heaven and earth,
The sea and all that is in them;
Who keeps truth forever;
7 Who does justice for the oppressed;
Who gives food to the hungry.
Yahweh sets the prisoners free.
8 Yahweh opens the eyes of the blind;
Yahweh raises up those who are bowed down;
Yahweh loves the righteous;
9 Yahweh keeps the sojourners;
He helps up the orphan and the widow,
But He bends the way of the wicked.

10 Yahweh will reign forever,
Your God, O Zion, from generation to generation.
Praise Yah![90]

That's the Word of God.

When is the last time that you were counting on someone for help and they disappointed you? Probably sometime very recently. Let me ask the question even more forcefully: when is the last time you were disappointed with a *politician*? Someone that you voted for and you thought for sure that was going to be the guy or the gal who was going to do everything right that needed to be done, and so forth? And it turned out, guess what? It didn't work out quite that way. Well, we have all had that kind of an experience of disappointment in another person, maybe because of a promise that wasn't kept or a problem that wasn't solved. Or in many cases, perhaps a failure of character, especially for someone who's in a position of church leadership, for example.

This kind of common experience is going to help amplify the message that we have today in this psalm. And it is that it's vain for us to put our hopes in men, no matter how powerful they may be by human standards. And why is that? Because the most powerful men all pass away. And this is true whether they exercise their power for good or evil. So the twofold

[90] Ps 146 (LSB). Quoted again afterward.

message goes like this: that we should not place false hopes in the *good* leader, nor should we despair under the yoke of a *bad* one—because both alike will pass away, along with all their power and along with all their plans.

This psalm is here to remind us that God reigns over all. He is the source of all encouragement. And that means for the present and for the future. He is the only sure hope because he is the one who inhabits eternity. He is the unchanging one and he's the unchangeable one. So today let's consider this psalm. Ten verses in four parts. And I've tried to make these a little more memorable for you today.

The first is a call to *worship*. Worship. Secondly, a *warning* against putting our trust in princes. Thirdly, the *wisdom* of trusting in God. And fourthly, the *warranty* of God's everlasting dominion.

Worship, warning, wisdom, and warranty.

We like to start with a little background. This is an interesting psalm because it begins the last series of five psalms in the Psalter that are all worship psalms. They're called *Hallel* psalms, in fact, which you might wonder if that's where we get that word, *hallelujah*, because it literally means *praise Yahweh*. And that's how it's translated in the *Legacy*

Standard version here, *praise Yah*. We do well to remember—because it's one of those words that we may use in a lot of different situations—that it does include God's name and therefore we need to be careful how we use it. Spurgeon reminded us that the irreverent use of this word (hallelujah)is *an aggravated instance of taking the name of Jehovah our God in vain*. So we should be careful how we use it.

These praise psalms, we could say are a fitting capstone to the Psalter. As we go through the psalms, we are plumbing, as it were, the depths of human despair. We may soar at times on the heights of inexpressible joy in the Psalter. And then that collection of songs ends by turning to the praise of God who lives and reigns forever.

We don't know in this case who wrote the psalm. We think it was written about 500 B.C., towards the end of the Old Testament era, or the time of the writing of the last Old Testament scriptures. And it's worth being reminded how old this psalm is, 2,500 years old, because why? Because we live in the same kind of time. We have the same kind of struggles. God's word does not change with the passage of time. Nor does our need for God's mercy. God's word is always timeless. And we can say that it's timeless because it is *the eternal word of God*. It is *written in the heavens*.

So let's consider the first two verses, the call to *worship*.

1 Praise Yah!
Praise Yahweh, O my soul!
2 I will praise Yahweh throughout my life;
I will sing praises to my God while I have my being.

And we see in these first two verses, two *exhortations* of worship. And we also see two *conditions* of worship. The two exhortations are first of all, for *everyone* to praise God. And then interestingly enough, the psalmist calls *himself* to praise God. He's calling others and then he's calling himself. And the two conditions, we should notice that it's first of all, praise for the *present* life, but then also praise for the life to *come*. And it seems that this psalm has sort of a circular pattern to it, that it begins with praise in anticipation. It begins with anticipation and it's going to be followed with gratitude. In other words, the psalmist begins with praise, and he begins to meditate upon God, and that meditation on God drives him back at the end of the psalm to praise once again, so that it begins and ends with praise.

Worship is personal. We need to remember that worship is an *individual* activity. And that's true even when we're worshiping in the assembly on occasions like this. No man can worship for another. Each man has to worship for himself. And true worship, as Jesus tells us, is *in spirit and in truth*, where each one is worshiping the *true* God, and each one is worshiping through the *spiritual bond* that the believer has with his Creator. So the conditions for proper worship is that it must be according to the *truth* of God—and we find that in the Bible—and that it can only come properly from a soul that has been renewed by the *Spirit* of God. Because spiritually dead men can only worship idols, and such worship is never pleasing to God.

Worship is not only personal, but it's also *perpetual* for this life and for the next. Our worship in this life is designed to be a foretaste of the worship that we'll offer God in the next life. And that what is temporary and imperfect in this life, in the next life will be perfect and perpetual. We might wonder at times whether in eternity—we like to sing that song *when we've been there for 10,000 years, we have no less days to sing his praise*—whether, after 10,000 years, are we going to get bored? Or at some point, maybe 100,000, or a million? And the answer of course is *no*. We'll *never* tire of worshiping our God.

The commentator H.C. Leupold says this:

> Those individuals who have made derisive remarks about the monotony of eternal praise of God, know not whereof they speak.

And if you're like me, you've probably had to suffer through at least one of those sermons in your life.

This pattern of praise is going to give us a pattern for *life*. What is that? It is that whatever we do, we do it all to the glory of God. And in this way, all of our life becomes a form of worship. He has made us for this very purpose: to bring glory to him in this life and in the next. Psalm 115 reminds us:

> Not to us, O Yahweh, not to us,
> But to Your name give glory
> Because of Your lovingkindness, because of Your truth.[91]

In the next two verses, let's consider the folly of trusting in princes. The psalmist says:

> 3 Do not trust in nobles,
> In merely a son of man, in whom there is no salvation.
> 4 His spirit departs, he returns to the earth;
> In that very day his plans perish.

Is it the case that men help one another? And the answer is, of course. And if there's some truth to that, then why is the psalmist in this instance so adamant about warning us about trusting in man? We'll think about it this way—that first of all, there is no *complete* help in trusting in man, and that there's no *lasting* help in trusting man, and especially—and this is where we're going—that there is no *ultimate* help in man.

---

[91] Ps 115:1 (LSB).

Some months ago when we were studying Psalm 49, we were reminded that one man cannot ransom another one. Let me quote that from Psalm 49. It says:

> 7 Truly, no man can redeem his brother;
> He cannot give to God a ransom for him—
> 8 For the redemption price for their soul is costly,
> And it ceases forever—
> 9 That he should live on eternally,
> That he should not see corruption.[92]

One man cannot ransom the life of another. But if, just for instance, if we were to put our trust in men, wouldn't it be the strongest—those who have earthly power—kings, princes? But if it's the case that the strongest have no power to help us, then what folly is there in trusting in anyone at all?

Let me also make this quite clear, because we don't want to get the idea that somehow this means that instead of trusting in someone else, you should trust in *yourself*. That's a very vogue idea today, that you can only trust in yourself. But that is not what the psalmist is saying here. It is not a call to *self-reliance*. Quite on the contrary—because frankly, if you were already sufficient in and of yourself, you would not need to be warned not to trust in princes.

---

[92] Ps 49:7-9 (LSB).

Psalm 118 echoes the same idea:

> 8 It is better to take refuge in Yahweh
> Than to trust in man.
> 9 It is better to take refuge in Yahweh
> Than to trust in nobles.[93]

The message here is that such a reliance on man is as dangerous as laying hold of a millstone as a life preserver. I promise you're going to be disappointed with the results.

Verse four is expressing the reality that man himself is nothing more—this is kind of funny actually—nothing more than dirt plus wind, dirt plus wind, body and spirit. The expression here, *son of man*, literally means *son of Adam* or *son of the earth*, because Adam was literally named for the dirt that God formed him out of at the beginning of creation. Man does not have the power to keep himself alive. He is not a reliable source of help, although he's often a reliable source of trouble. Nevertheless, the one who is a troublemaker, God will deal with in due time.

William Graham Scroggie says this:

> All the pomp and pageantry of the so-called great will be laid in the dust. All alike are mere men, weak men, helpless men,

[93] Ps 118:8-9 (LSB).

> mortal men, corruptible men, perishing men. To trust men instead of trusting God is dishonoring to God, degrading to him who does so, and always disappointing.

At the conclusion of this message, we're also going to see why we must not place our trust in religious leaders. We're going to see that there is only one man, the God man, Jesus, who can stand before God on our behalf.

What does this passage tell us about our own plans? We like to make plans, but there are several warnings here. First of all, if the plans are merely our own, they will come to nothing, that anything we try to do on our own strength is going to fail, that only those plans that align with God will stand, and that anything we do against the will of God is going to be turned against us in the end.

We might agree that man could be of a little help in this life, a little bit, but we need to remember that he is no help at all for the life to come because the psalm is speaking both in terms of the present and the future. The present worship and future worship as we've seen, and then present deliverance from temporal troubles, and then the ultimate deliverance, which is the deliverance from the kingdom of darkness into the kingdom of God's Son. We'll see this connection a little more clearly in the next section.

While I don't like to incorporate too many quotes because it can be a little bit distracting, there are several short quotes that I want to share with you as we conclude this second section. The first is by John King, who says:

> The psalmist, if you mark it, climbs up by degrees to the disabling of the best men amongst us and in them all the rest.

You get that, right? That if the best, the strongest, the wisest cannot be of any help, then no one lesser can be of help either. Nathaniel Hardy says:

> Nothing is more foolish than to build on the sand, giving trust to men whose persons together with their thoughts perish in a moment.

And we know how transient men can be. Joseph Caryl says:

> Those words *in whom there is no help* are not a distinction of weak princes from strong ones, but a conclusion that there is no help in the strongest.

And Spurgeon, who's one of our favorites, says:

> Men are always far too apt to depend upon the great ones of earth and forget the great one above.

That is where we need to turn our attention next. The *wisdom* of trusting in God, verses five through nine.

> 5 How blessed is he whose help is the God of Jacob,
> Whose hope is in Yahweh his God,
> 6 Who made heaven and earth,
> The sea and all that is in them;
> Who keeps truth forever;
> 7 Who does justice for the oppressed;
> Who gives food to the hungry.
> Yahweh sets the prisoners free.
> 8 Yahweh opens the eyes of the blind;
> Yahweh raises up those who are bowed down;
> Yahweh loves the righteous;
> 9 Yahweh keeps the sojourners;
> He helps up the orphan and the widow,
> But He bends the way of the wicked.

Here we see that God is both a present help and a future hope. And why is that? Because salvation has to be under the words of this psalm at this point. Now in this section, we're reminded that God is the Creator and that occurs quite often throughout the scriptures. When God is about to make an important point, he starts oftentimes by saying, *I'm the one who made heaven and earth*. Why such emphasis?

H.C. Leupold says it this way:

> It must be quite obvious that he who has made can control what he has made.

And Spurgeon says:

> The making of the worlds is the standing proof of the power and wisdom of that great God in whom we trust.

So we have this assurance that God who created the heavens and earth is not disconnected from, and he is not disinterested in, the world that he has made. In this section, the God of all creation is also called *the God of Jacob*. Now, if you know something about the life of Jacob, that ought to be a little funny because the word *Jacob* refers to Jacob's actions toward his brother of attempting to supplant or supersede his older brother. In other words, he was a deceiver. He was a trickster. And here is God taking the name *Jacob* upon himself. He's identifying so closely with his people that he identifies himself according to the name of Jacob, whose life was for the most part, not exemplary, let's say. This is the God who stoops down to take the name of his stubborn people. And it's also the God whom we can call *our* God. He belongs to us and we belong to him.

Yahweh comes to the aid of the oppressed and he overthrows the power of the wicked. And as he does that, he demonstrates both his goodness and his strength. And it's a strength that no man can match. God makes a clear distinction. We see lots of distinctions and contrasts in our study of the psalms. God is here making a distinction between those who belong to him and those who are his enemies. And we're reminded of how he spoke to Pharaoh as he was preparing to deliver his people Israel out of their bondage in Egypt. He says to Pharaoh, *I will make a distinction between your people and my people*. And that is how God deals with man in terms of those distinctions.

This psalm picks up on the language of *setting prisoners free* and *giving sight to the blind*. And that's used as a frequent metaphor in the Old Testament for salvation.

Listen to what Isaiah says in chapter 42:

> Thus says the God, Yahweh,
> Who created the heavens and stretched them out,
> Who spread out the earth and its offspring,
> Who gives breath to the people on it
> And spirit to those who walk in it,
> "I am Yahweh, I have called You in righteousness . . . .

And he's referring to Jesus here.

> "I am Yahweh, I have called You in righteousness;
> I will also take hold of You by the hand and guard You,
> And I will give You as a covenant to the people,
> As a light to the nations,
> To open blind eyes,

> To bring out prisoners from the dungeon
> And those who inhabit darkness from the prison.

Referring to the work of Jesus.

> "I am Yahweh, that is My name;
> I will not give My glory to another,
> Nor My praise to graven images."[94]

Jesus quotes Isaiah in the New Testament at the beginning of his ministry, that he is the one who's going to do this. Listen to what he says. This is from Luke chapter four:

> And He came to Nazareth, where He had been brought up, and as was His custom, He entered the synagogue on the Sabbath and stood up to read.
>
> And the scroll of the prophet Isaiah was handed to Him. And He opened the scroll and found the place where it was written,
>
> "THE SPIRIT OF THE LORD IS UPON ME,
> BECAUSE HE ANOINTED ME TO PREACH THE GOSPEL TO THE POOR.
> HE HAS SENT ME TO PROCLAIM RELEASE TO THE CAPTIVES,
> AND RECOVERY OF SIGHT TO THE BLIND,
> TO SET FREE THOSE WHO ARE OPPRESSED,
> TO PROCLAIM THE FAVORABLE YEAR OF THE LORD."

[94] Is 42:5-8 (LSB).

> And He closed the scroll, gave it back to the attendant and sat down, and the eyes of all in the synagogue were fixed on Him. And He began to say to them, "Today this Scripture has been fulfilled in your hearing."[95]

We need this kind of confidence—especially when the wicked seem to prosper, and they often do—because we live in a fallen, cursed world. We need this confidence that God will always turn the wicked designs for his good purpose. Isaiah says this in chapter 40:

> It is He who reduces rulers to nothing,
> Who makes the judges of the earth utterly formless.
> Scarcely have they been planted;
> Scarcely have they been sown;
> Scarcely has their stem taken root in the earth,
> But He merely blows on them, and they wither,
> And the storm carries them away like stubble.[96]

Why would you want to put your trust in princes if they are that easily overthrown?

Wicked men can only devise evil, that is what they do. But God can only work good from those evil deeds.

---

[95] Luke 4:16-21 (LSB).

[96] Is 40:23-24 (LSB).

Listen to what Scroggie says:

> What a comfort it is to know that God overthrows the plans and defeats the schemes of the wicked. He makes evil designs subservient to higher and better ends.

There's at least a threefold application of this general principle that man's designs come to nothing. First, we've already heard this, *we mustn't trust in princes*. Secondly, that *God catches the crafty and their deception*. And the encouragement for those who are struggling under any kind of oppression is that thirdly, *God turns their evil for good*. There's also a principle here that if the most powerful men cannot deliver us from temporal afflictions, the afflictions of this life, then they certainly can't deliver us from eternal afflictions. If we're going to be saved from sin, we're going to need something more than a mere man to do that. Nor can a man deliver himself. Man has to look to God for his deliverance. And that's true even for kings, the most powerful. Even the king must look to God for his deliverance. He must not trust in his own wisdom or in the strength of his armies, as it says elsewhere. *Do not trust in chariots and horses*, which is what kings often do. They think their strength somehow protects them.

Lastly, we're going to consider the certainty of God's dominion. This is the final verse, verse 10.

> 10 Yahweh will reign forever,
> Your God, O Zion, from generation to generation.
> Praise Yah!

Worship is a fitting response to our meditation upon God's goodness, because the one who lives and reigns forever is worthy of all of our praise and thanksgiving. Now, if it's the case, as we have seen, that a mere man cannot be trusted, then whom do we trust? And the answer is that Christ is that man. He is the better prince. He is the prince of peace who reigns forever. And he's also that better priest, who ever lives to make intercession at the right hand of God. This is how the writer of Hebrews puts it in chapter seven:

> And the former priests, on the one hand, existed in greater numbers because they were prevented by death from continuing, but Jesus, on the other hand, because He continues forever, holds His priesthood permanently. Therefore He is able also to save forever those who draw near to God through Him, since He always lives to make intercession for them.
>
> For it was fitting for us to have such a high priest, holy, innocent, undefiled, separated from sinners and exalted above the heavens; who does not need daily, like those high priests, to offer up sacrifices, first for His own sins and then for the sins of the people, because this He did once for all when He offered up Himself. For the Law appoints men as high priests who are weak, but the word of the oath, which came after the Law, appoints a Son, who has been made perfect forever.[97]

[97] Heb 7:23-28 (LSB).

Zion's God is our God through the Son of God, Jesus Christ. Listen carefully. Put your trust in the great Prince and High Priest who lives forever. He has made the only way for you to be reconciled to God. By his own life and death, he puts away your sin so that it is remembered no more forever. As high as heaven is from the earth, and as far as the east is from the west, so far has he taken away your sin by his shed blood, so that you can now be reckoned adopted sons and daughters of God, heirs of his kingdom and co-heirs with Christ. And that having received such a great gift by faith, let your heart turn to him in unending praise.

The pastor and theologian Jim Boice said it like this:

> Praise is where all true religious contemplation should end up. Particularly as our lives move toward their inevitable earthly ends, they should be full of praise.

Is that your confidence? If so, then praise Yahweh.

Amen.

Heavenly Father, we ask that you would apply these words to our hearts and our minds today. Bring all of your people to yourself through this call of the word and through the call of the Spirit. Justify them and sanctify them in the truth. Help them to lift their praises to you both now and forever. In Christ's name and for his glory. Amen.

The Madness of Atheism (Psalm 14)

November 12, 2023

Our message today comes from Psalm 14, and I'll be reading from the *Legacy Standard Bible*. There are seven verses here. It's a fairly short psalm.

Listen carefully as we begin to look at the word of God today:

1 The wicked fool says in his heart, "There is no God."
They act corruptly, they commit abominable deeds;
There is no one who does good.
2 Yahweh looks down from heaven upon the sons of men
To see if there is anyone who has insight,
Anyone who seeks after God.
3 They have all turned aside, altogether they have become worthless;
There is no one who does good, not even one.

4 Do all the workers of iniquity not know,
Who eat up my people as they eat bread,
And do not call upon Yahweh?
5 There they are in great dread,
For God is with the righteous generation.
6 You would put to shame the counsel of the afflicted,
But Yahweh is his refuge.

7 Oh, that the salvation of Israel would come out of Zion!
When Yahweh restores His captive people,
May Jacob rejoice, may Israel be glad.[98]

This is the word of God.

We've talked on several occasions now as we've worked our way through the psalms of how the psalms describe the condition of man in his fallenness. Just as we were praying a moment ago, we are surrounded by evidence of atheism because we live in a violent world and a turbulent world—a world that has rejected God and embraced every kind of evil. We can't help but find ourselves to be shocked and saddened by stories of violence and cruelty. But the Bible tells us in very graphic terms that fallen man is at enmity with God. He is enemies of God. He hates God and he hates his fellow man. And this is nothing new because this has been true since Adam and Eve rebelled in the Garden of Eden. And time, as we see, has not improved man's spiritual condition. Consequently, the verdict is that we are all born atheists and misanthropes, hating God and hating one another.

We have to be careful at this point not to be misled by the idea that man still has some goodness left in him because even man at his very *best* is still under judgment. There's no one that can please God by his own

[98] Ps 14 (LSB). Quoted again afterward.

efforts. And man, when we see him at his *worst*, is a devil who is busy trying to destroy everything that God creates. He is determined to wreck anything that demonstrates the reality of God. He is determined, as well, to do *evil* and to call it *good*. He has to try to excuse himself for his wickedness and try to turn it into virtue. And yet he ends up driving himself mad trying to reshape the world according to the deformed pattern that he finds within himself.

As I mentioned, we have repeatedly seen how plainly and graphically the psalms speak of man's fallen nature. And as well, how the psalms are used in the New Testament to make this point with considerable force, as we will see again today.

We'll consider this psalm in its three natural divisions and I'll use the letter C to help make it a little more memorable.

The first is the *craziness* of the atheist. Second is the *cruelty* of the atheist. And third is the *confidence* of the righteous.

And we like to take a moment to do a little bit of background on the psalm. It has a heading that states that it is for the *choir director* and it is *a psalm of David*. So it's attributed to David, which places it at about

3,000 years ago. And we see the occasion is that it's been composed for congregational singing.

And interestingly, Psalm 14 has a virtual twin. Psalm 53 is almost identical to this psalm. There's only a slight variation that we find in the fifth and sixth verses. Not only that, but we see part of this psalm is repeated in the New Testament, in the third chapter of Romans. And as well, we're going to use this New Testament passage, this usage, to help make the meaning of it clear. In other words, what we're going to be looking at today in Psalm 14 is not a new understanding of this psalm because this is exactly how Paul is going to use it in his letter to the Romans.

We know when the Spirit continues to repeat things over and over again that it must be important. And there's at least a threefold repetition of this idea to demonstrate the importance of this doctrine. We want to make sure that we understand just how severe the condition of man is after the Fall. And the simple reason is that if we don't understand the severity of the illness, we'll not be prepared to receive the cure. What we're seeing is an outworking of the enmity between Christ and Satan. It goes all the way back to the Garden of Eden, when God says to the serpent, *I will put enmity between your seed and her seed*. So we live in that time between the Fall in the Garden and the fulfillment of the redemptive promises at the end of this age, where there will continue to be this spiritual warfare.

Let's first consider the *craziness* of the atheist. The first three verses:

> 1 The wicked fool says in his heart, "There is no God."
> They act corruptly, they commit abominable deeds;
> There is no one who does good.
> 2 Yahweh looks down from heaven upon the sons of men
> To see if there is anyone who has insight,
> Anyone who seeks after God.
> 3 They have all turned aside, altogether they have become worthless;
> There is no one who does good, not even one.

That's the opening of this psalm. Now here I want to share a quotation from the Prince of Preachers, Charles Spurgeon, who has this to say: that *atheism is a strange thing*. He says, *even the devils never fell into that vice*. Or as we read in James 2:19, *the devils believe and tremble*. How is it then that man can take this extraordinary view that there is no God? This thing that we call atheism is really just a false hope in a non-existent God who cannot and will not judge sin. That's the gist of it. It is man in his fallenness wanting to justify himself by distancing himself from God.

The translation that we're looking at today adds a modifier to this. It calls the fool *wicked*, the *wicked fool*. And that helps us understand that atheism is a moral problem and not an intellectual problem. It's not a question of examining the evidence and deciding that there's not enough evidence for God. It's a rejection of God on moral grounds. And even the word that we use here, *atheism*, is a little misleading. It might be more accurate to call it anti-*theism*. Or anti-*Godism*. There is an opposition to God. And then by this, we have to understand that when we say anti-*God*, we mean anti-*God-of-the-Bible*, or anti-*Yahweh*, or if you prefer a more familiar way of putting it, anti-*Christ*.

We usually use that latter expression as a way of associating with the Devil, but it has much broader meaning because there are two categories in this world. There are those who are *for* Christ and then all the rest who are *against* him, no matter how religious they may claim to be. And that's an important point that we need to understand—that the atheist, so-called, is actually quite religious. But his religion is a rejection of the one true and living God. So in this respect, we can say that fallen man does not seek God. He is running from God and chasing after idols of his own imagination. So here's a very important point: that atheism, in spite of arguments to the contrary, is a religious commitment. It is an expression of profound faith, even though it's being framed in the negative.

There are many different kinds of atheists. We're using that term very broadly. The atheist is not necessarily one who simply tries to claim that there is no God. And even in this psalm where it opens with that line that *the wicked fool says in his heart, there is no God*, we understand that he's actually lying when he says that. He knows there is a God. He's trying to convince himself and others that there is no God. So this is someone who is defiant and someone who is passionate in his opposition to God.

There are those of an intellectual sort who will try to argue for their atheism by saying that science somehow explains everything. And they're satisfied that science can do that sort of thing, no matter how much faith it may take. And there's a particularly famous man named Richard Dawkins, who's actually written books about this, one called, *The God Delusion*. And when asked on one occasion in an interview, what is he going to do if he comes face to face with God one day? How is he going to answer his atheism? His response is that he's going to say to God, *why didn't you show yourself?* Now that's a very brazen thing to say because he makes it sound as if God either hasn't provided any evidence of his existence or that whatever evidence he's provided isn't enough. It doesn't meet his standard. And either way, we notice that it's, guess what? It's the atheist who is judging the evidence to be inadequate.

Is there proof of God's existence? And the answer is of course. God is known through all of his creation—from the very highest to the very lowest thing, whether it's something complex and beautiful or whether it's something simple, even a rock, because nothing at all could exist apart from him. So there's not a problem of a lack of evidence. The problem is an unwillingness to acknowledge the evidence that's there, and a demand by the creature that God must meet his standard of proof.

The funny thing is, if you've studied your Bible, you realize that God has to hide his glory from mankind in order to spare man from an instantaneous death. He would not even allow Moses to see his face, but placed Moses in the cleft of the rock so that Moses would not be exposed to his full glory. It's also true that God has revealed himself through the person of Jesus Christ. He has come in the flesh. He has dwelt among us. And it's also the case that he's going to reveal himself at the end of the age when Christ returns. And it's also true that he's revealed himself in other ways, such as through his word. God's existence is known through his creation. His creation demonstrates his power. God's salvation is known through his Son and through his Spirit. And the knowledge of salvation comes to us through the reading and the preaching of the Bible, God's written word, which we easily take for granted, and which we also notice the atheist automatically rejects and says, *this is not sufficient evidence*. So who is it that really has more faith? Is it the atheist who believes that everything came from nothing for no reason? Or is it the Christian who believes that God made the heavens and the earth to show forth his glory? Can *nothing* create *anything*? And if not, can it create *everything*? And the answer, of course, is *no* in both cases.

Some years ago, there was a TV personality—a scientist named Carl Sagan—who had a show called *Cosmos*. And at the beginning of that show, he expressed his own faith with the following statement. He said that *the cosmos is all that is or was or ever will be*. And in stating that, he's stating his own faith that there is no God. That is the atheist creed, you might say. Is that true? Can it be true? And the answer is *no*, that neither science nor reason allow for the possibility that the cosmos is *all that is*. And then we have to come to the following conclusion, which is a little uncomfortable, that the atheist is a *liar*. He is morally defective. We could say that he is of his father, the devil, who is a liar, and the father of lies, just as Jesus said of the Pharisees. The atheist is in fact a rebel who has set himself against the knowledge and the wisdom of God in order to pursue his own evil intentions.

I want you to understand something. The atheist is trying to play a mind game. He's trying to engage in a parlor trick because he wants to make a difference between you, the one who has religion, and himself who doesn't have religion. He doesn't want you to see that his atheism is a religious belief that is just as dogmatic as any other religious belief. And this is part of what makes him a liar. He wants to claim that he is not religious and that his non-religion is actually morally and intellectually superior to your outdated belief in God. The psalmist therefore calls him a *wicked fool* without exaggerating the case. The atheist is the one who's standing on a mountain of evidence for God and trying to claim that it doesn't exist and it can't be found.

That's bad enough, but I've got worse news than that. The bad news about atheism is that the Bible is telling us that we are all born in this condition. It is universal, it's not unusual. It's not the exception. The psalmist says that God is looking down from heaven and finds absolutely no one who does good, no one who seeks God among the whole human race. And the apostle Paul is going to pick up on this idea and make the case with irrefutable force in the opening chapter of Romans. We're going to be looking at some excerpts from the first three chapters of Romans.

First of all, Paul is going to show that all men know God from his creation. Quoting from chapter one, Paul says:

> . . . that which is known about God is evident within them; for God made it evident to them. For since the creation of the world His invisible attributes, both His eternal power and divine

> nature, have been clearly seen, being understood through what has been made, so that they are without excuse.[99]

And here we can almost hear Paul quoting from the 19th Psalm, which opens like this:

> 1 The heavens are telling of the glory of God;
> And the expanse is declaring the work of His hands.
> 2 Day to day pours forth speech,
> And night to night reveals knowledge.
> 3 There is no speech, nor are there words;
> Their voice is not heard.
> 4 Their line has gone out through all the earth,
> And their utterances to the end of the world.[100]

In other words, the creation itself is speaking in a universal language that all men everywhere can see and understand. There's kind of a paradox here of what it's calling silent speech. Nature doesn't have to utter a word in order to reveal the knowledge of God because the heavens tell the glory of God.

This is very interesting: that God in this psalm is directing man's attention skyward to an expanse that is so far beyond his reach that he can't even begin to comprehend it. Even today with the most modern

---

[99] Rom 1:19-20 (LSB).

[100] Ps 19:1-4 (LSB).

kinds of technology, we are only scratching the surface in terms of our understanding of the size and the complexity of the universe. And no matter how far we may see into the edges of the universe, here's an interesting thought: that however large the universe may be—and we haven't figured that out yet—but no matter how big it is, God has to be bigger. God is bigger than his creation.

We also might notice that anything that's here on earth that a man can try to get his hands on, he's going to try to take credit for it. But not the stars. Look at the stars. You can't *reach* them. You can't even *count* them. These all belong to God, and he calls them all by name.

The prophet Isaiah says this:

> Lift up your eyes on high
> And see who has created these stars,
> The One who leads forth their host by number,
> He calls them all by name;
> Because of the greatness of His vigor and the strength of His power,
> Not one of them is missing.[101]

And remember, I said—it's true—we don't even know how many stars there are, but he knows them all. Not one of them is missing and he has

[101] Is 40:26 (LSB).

a name for each and every one of them. God sets the stars in heaven as a witness of his power and his glory. But wicked men reject even this knowledge of God. And what's worse, they worship the creation instead of worshiping the Creator. Paul picks up this thought in verse 21 of Romans 1:

> For even though they knew God, they did not glorify Him as God or give thanks, but they became futile in their thoughts, and their foolish heart was darkened. Professing to be wise, they became fools, and exchanged the glory of the incorruptible God for an image in the likeness of corruptible man and of birds and four-footed animals and crawling creatures.[102]

We might notice that there's another way that wicked men reject the knowledge of God that we find in nature, because it's plain that God made man *male and female*. And yet man rejects the natural attraction between male and female for what Paul describes as *dishonorable passions* which lead to indecent acts of lust. So even our very nature as male and female, man tries to deny and to suppress.

That's not the end of the verdict here, because those men who Paul says reject God are given over to a futile mind. They have abandoned true wisdom. They have lost their capacity for reason. In fact, they think that reality is whatever they imagine it to be. And this is a delusion that we

---

[102] Rom 1:21-23 (LSB).

call postmodern philosophy. It's an end game of futility because there are no answers in that kind of philosophy. And so in looking at this, we see that God ends up making foolish the wisdom of the world. What man thinks is so brilliant in terms of philosophy turns out to be nothing but foolishness. So we now begin to understand the craziness of the atheist. He is driven to madness and futility by his unreason as well as by his unnatural desires. He is trying to live against the reality of the world that God has made, but no matter how hard he tries, he cannot conform it to his own designs. By setting himself against the knowledge of God, the atheist is also separating himself from the salvation that is to be found only in Jesus Christ. He rejects the only remedy for his condition and then tries to save himself. And this too is an act of futility.

No man in such a desperate condition can save himself or make himself ready for salvation. In fact, the Bible says that he is *dead in sins and trespasses*, which tells us that he has to receive a supernatural work of new life in order to see and to enter into the kingdom of heaven.

In the second stanza of this psalm, we begin to see the *cruelty* of the atheist. Listen to verses four through six:

> 4 Do all the workers of iniquity not know,
> Who eat up my people as they eat bread,
> And do not call upon Yahweh?

> 5 There they are in great dread,
> For God is with the righteous generation.
> 6 You would put to shame the counsel of the afflicted,
> But Yahweh is his refuge.

If a man's mind and affections have been completely corrupted, as we saw in those opening verses, what can we expect him to *do*? What is going to be the outworking of that kind of corrupt affection? Or to put it another way, can a man who is evil on the inside be good on the outside? Or should we be surprised if such a man is capable of great wickedness? Now back to Romans 1. Paul warns us that every kind of sin follows from this fallen condition of man. Verse 29:

> . . . unrighteousness, wickedness, greed, evil; full of envy, murder, strife, deceit, malice; . . .

He goes on to list a number of other kinds of foolish wickedness in the next two verses. He says:

> . . . they are gossips, slanderers, haters of God, violent, arrogant, boastful, inventors of evil, disobedient to parents, without understanding, untrustworthy, unloving, unmerciful; . . .

And after reading these offenses, Paul goes on to give the verdict in verse 32:

> . . . and although they know the righteous requirement of God, that those who practice such things are worthy of death, they not only do the same, but also give hearty approval to those who practice them.[103]

So you see, they know there is a God. They know He is righteous. They know He judges the wicked. And they also know that the wicked deserve death.

Now that's just chapter one.

In chapter one, Paul is making his case for the wickedness of the Gentiles, those who are outside the community of Israel. And he's making that argument not from scripture, but from nature. So now Paul is going to deliver the second blow, as it were, right into the gut of his own people, using the very words of Yahweh from the scriptures to show not just the Gentiles, but that *all men of all kinds are all under the same judgment of sin.* His argument is going to open with a quotation from the psalm that we just read. Listen for it. He says:

> What then? Are we [Jews] better? Not at all; for we have already charged that both Jews and Greeks are all under sin; as it is written . . .

---

[103] Rom 1:29-32 (LSB)

And here it comes:

> "THERE IS NONE RIGHTEOUS, NOT EVEN ONE;
> THERE IS NONE WHO UNDERSTANDS,
> THERE IS NONE WHO SEEKS FOR GOD;
> ALL HAVE TURNED ASIDE, TOGETHER THEY HAVE BECOME WORTHLESS;
> THERE IS NONE WHO DOES GOOD,
> THERE IS NOT EVEN ONE."[104]

Paul ends up concluding his indictment by declaring that the whole world is guilty before God and there are no exceptions. That also means you. You are likewise that man who is without hope in the world. Paul says of those who now believe:

> . . . remember that you were *at that time* without Christ, *alienated* from the citizenship of Israel, and *strangers* to the covenants of promise, *having no hope and without God in the world.*[105] (emphasis added)

The problem of sin that we see described in the scripture is exactly what we see in the world around us. If we want to understand the violence, the wickedness, the chaos of the world we see, wars and all the rest, then we have to understand it in terms of man's spiritual condition. And if

[104] Rom 3:9-12 (LSB).

[105] Eph 2:12 (LSB).

we're honest enough, we're also going to say that we see the same things in our own hearts. Now this is bad news. Man is in such a condition that he should expect nothing but the judgment of God. Is that the end of the story? Thank goodness it's not. The psalm ends with a very hopeful strain.

The third point today is the *confidence* of the righteous. Verse seven:

> 7 Oh, that the salvation of Israel would come out of Zion!
> When Yahweh restores His captive people,
> May Jacob rejoice, may Israel be glad.

As we think about this last verse, let's ask a few questions. Who is Israel here? It's referring to God's chosen people, to those whom he chooses to reveal his mercy. What then is our captivity? It is that bondage to sin that is typified by Israel's captivity in the land of Egypt, the oppression and the affliction and a crying out for deliverance by divine intervention. And then what is our salvation? It's deliverance from the oppression, as strangers in a foreign land—as we remain—and the promise of a new land where God dwells with his people. Where's our hope in the midst of our present tribulations? That even though the journey is long and it's filled with hardship, the promises of God cannot fail. For his love for his people sustains them through every difficulty. And what then is the response? How can we remain confident when surrounded by enemies? And the answer is that we can praise God that he has made a difference by setting his love on us when we were his enemies. And we can have confidence that his mercy will deliver many others along the way, just as we were first delivered from our bondage. In other words, Christ is still building his church and adding to the number of those who are being saved.

We saw how using this psalm, Paul laid out the bad news of man's fallen condition before God, but that's not the end of the story by any stretch. What else does he have to say? Paul also says that there's a righteousness that is apart from the works of the law. He calls it the righteousness of faith, and that it is the basis on which God justifies the wicked—so that there is now no condemnation for those who are in Christ Jesus, for those who trust in him for deliverance from the bondage of sin and for adoption as sons and daughters of God who are now heirs of the kingdom. And not only that, but that no powers of wickedness in heaven or on earth can separate such a one from the love of God in Christ Jesus.

Does that sound like good news? That sounds like really good news! That's the gospel. The good news that while we were yet sinners, enemies of God, Christ died for the ungodly to purchase for himself a people for his own glory. And that by trusting in him, they will all receive the gift of eternal life, not by works so that no man may boast, but by faith in the one who has accomplished everything necessary to reconcile God to his enemies, the one having lived a perfect life and having died as a substitute.

As we bring our thoughts today to a conclusion, we can circle back and ask the question, *does the atheist really believe there is no God?* The answer is, of course not. His words and actions reflect that he knows there is a God. How so? It's paradoxical: that the hatred and violence of the atheist demonstrates that he knows there is a God and that God will judge all men. It's the very judgment of God that men hate and fight against. It is the righteousness of God that the wicked see in the redeemed, which they fear. They are indeed without excuse and will stand judged unless they seek the mercy of God in Christ.

I want to give you an exhortation at this point and go back to Paul again. This time, Paul is addressing an assembly in the city of Athens. Having walked through the city and seen that the city was overtaken by idols, he stands and addresses the Athenians and has this to say to them:

> "The God who made the world and all things in it, since He is Lord of heaven and earth, does not dwell in temples made with hands; nor is He served by human hands, as though He needed anything, since He Himself gives to all people life and breath and all things; and He made from one man every nation of mankind to inhabit all the face of the earth, having determined their appointed times and the boundaries of their habitation,

> that they would seek God, if perhaps they might grope for Him and find Him, though He is not far from each one of us."[106]

God is close if we would have Him. We look at this psalm and say, *what do we do?* What should we do in response to this psalm? There are actually a number of answers to that question. We could summarize them as follows.

The first is to call upon God. That we should seek him while he may be found, that we should seek refuge in him, both for the present and for the future, that we should do good, that we should love God and we should love man, that we should cease to do evil, to walk in obedience to his law, and that we should rejoice in God's mercy and give him the glory that is due to his name, and not as the pagans who live in fear, because our confidence is in God and man can do no harm to our soul.

Now the former times of ignorance God overlooked have passed by. God now commands all men to repent and to believe the gospel. Today is the day of salvation. And if you do not yet trust Christ, then hear his voice. Do not harden your hearts against the great mercy of God that's offered to you. Know that God has drawn near to us through Christ and that none who trust in him will ever be put to shame.

---

[106] Acts 17:24-27 (LSB).

This is what Jesus said:

> "Come to Me, all who are weary and heavy-laden, and I will give you rest. Take My yoke upon you and learn from Me, for I am gentle and humble in heart, and YOU WILL FIND REST FOR YOUR SOULS. For My yoke is easy and My burden is light."[107]

Amen.

Father, as we consider the word that you've given us today, I pray that you would apply it to every heart and mind and spirit here, that any who is listening who does not know Christ savingly, that you would give him saving knowledge of Christ and bring him into the kingdom of your dear Son. We pray it in his name. Amen.

[107] Matt 11:28-30 (LSB).

Four Songs for Christmas (Luke 1-2)

December 10, 2023

Our message today, I'm calling *Four Songs for Christmas*. We just finished singing a few songs, didn't we? And we'll have at least one more to finish at the end. Now, one of the reasons why I think Christmas is my favorite time of the year is in part because of the music that we sing at this time of the year. In fact, I would say that some of my earliest memories of worship music are Christmas carols. And that's probably true for many of you as well. Now lately, in part, because of the turbulence of our world, I find myself listening to Christmas carols long *before* Thanksgiving and even several weeks *after* Christmas. So I'll mention that for your benefit, if you need permission to do the same.

Of course, any time of the year is a good time to sing about the Savior's birth. And it's the case that I had a pastor years ago who used to say that *every Sunday is Easter and Christmas*. So we can sing those songs at any time of the year. But there's something special about singing them at this time of the year. I don't think there's any time of the year that has so much music associated with it like Christmas does. In fact, that association is so strong that the season would seem strange without it, without that music surrounding us. Now we might first think of all of the *sacred* music like what we've just recently sung, but there's also lots of *popular* music that goes along with this season of the year. And we also add an assortment of things like colorful lights and decorations that help add to the brightness of what can be very long and dark days of winter. Now whatever we might think about the Christmas holiday, whether as a religious tradition or as a commercial enterprise—which unfortunately it has become—we cannot separate the season from the music.

Over this last year, we've been studying a number of the psalms. And it's helpful to remember as we read through the Psalter, that this book is a collection of inspired poetry that was originally meant to be sung by God's people. So it's not just *poetry*, but it's also a *song book*. And the book of psalms is not the only place that we find inspired song in the Bible. In fact, there are inspired songs throughout the scriptures from beginning to end. Now there's a pattern that it's always been the practice of God's people to sing his praises. And music is often used as a remembrance of his works to commemorate some special occasion and to give us a way to bring those special operations of God back to mind again. Music is meant to be sung as *worship* and it's also formulated as music to help us *remember* it, like many of the songs that we've just sung.

Singing is one of the highest forms of worship because of the way that it engages all of our faculties of mind, heart, and spirit. And it's also given to us as a means of encouragement, both to ourselves and to each other. So with that in mind, should it be any surprise that we should find both men and angels singing the praises of God upon the fulfillment of his promises regarding the advent of Christ? And of course, we shouldn't be surprised. In fact, it's more accurate to say that at this very moment in redemptive history, that it would be impossible for the creation to restrain its praises. For an occasion like this, you *know* that there's going to be music. Now, if the Old Testament saints were accustomed to singing about God's deliverance from Egypt, then the New Testament saints must surely sing about the fulfillment of that event that's pointing forward to Jesus Christ. So today we're going to look and see how song accompanies the arrival of the promised Son of God.

An important detail, as we look at these four songs, is that three of these songs quote from the Old Testament. And the fourth song actually comes directly from heaven. So these are words that are certainly inspired. Two of these texts have been set to music many times, as we'll see. And hopefully we'll be able to sing one of these at the conclusion of the message today. So here are the four songs that we'll consider. They're found in the first two chapters in the gospel of Luke. First of all, *Mary's song*. Then we have *Zechariah's song*. Both of those are found in chapter one of Luke. And then we'll look at *the song of the angels*, as well as *Simeon's song*, in the second chapter of Luke.

Since we're going to be looking at portions of scripture today, there's not a single reading of text that we will begin with. I will read those passages as we come to them. Luke's gospel has the most detailed account of the birth narrative. So it's often the case that we're turning to those two chapters at the beginning of Luke at this time of the year. I'm looking at how Luke unfolds the birth and the early life of Christ.

Some background that's important for us to realize at this particular moment in history is that for 400 years, God has been silent. There has been no prophecy, no word from God for 400 years until this event comes. And then the news that breaks forth at this time, of course, is that there will be a fulfillment of God's promises going all the way back to Adam and Eve.

We'll start by looking at *Mary's song*. When Mary is visited by the angel Gabriel, he makes this remarkable promise to her. We find it in the first chapter of Luke, starting in verse 30:

> And the angel said to her, "Do not be afraid, Mary, for you have found favor with God. And behold, you will conceive in your womb and bear a son, and you shall name Him Jesus. He will be great and will be called the Son of the Most High, and the Lord God will give Him the throne of His father David, and He will

> reign over the house of Jacob forever, and there will be no end of His kingdom."[108]

Remember that we had already been told that Mary at this point was betrothed to Joseph and that Joseph was a man of the house of David, and David was of the tribe of Judah. And we bring to mind the remarkable promise that God made to David. Remember that David desired to build a house for God. And God said, *nope, you're not going to build a house for me. Your son's going to build a house for me, but I'm going to build your house*. And he meant that in a figurative way. He says, *your house and your kingdom shall endure before me forever. Your throne shall be established forever*. Immediately following that, David prays to God, and though it's not presented as a song, it could probably be one because it is a song of praise or a word of praise where he says:

> So now, O Yahweh God, the word that You have spoken concerning Your slave and concerning his house, establish it forever, and do as You have spoken, that Your name may be magnified forever, by saying, 'Yahweh of hosts is God over Israel'; and the house of Your servant David shall be established before You.[109]

---

[108] Luke 1:30-33 (LSB).

[109] 2 Sam 7:25-26 (LSB).

All of this is background to Mary's song. And by going back to David, of course, we're going back a thousand years from where we are at this moment in history.

Six months before Mary is visited by the angel, that same angel, Gabriel, appeared to Zechariah the priest and promised that his wife, Elizabeth—remember both of them were in their old age—that she would bear a son and that he would be like the prophet Elijah, who would prepare the way for the coming Messiah. And that his name would be John. In chapter one of Luke, verses 15 and 17, we see this:

> For he will be great in the sight of the Lord; and HE WILL NOT DRINK ANY WINE OR STRONG DRINK, and he will be filled with the Holy Spirit while yet in his mother's womb. . . . And he will go before Him in the spirit and power of Elijah, TO TURN THE HEARTS OF THE FATHERS BACK TO THE CHILDREN, and the disobedient to the attitude of the righteous, to make ready a people prepared for the Lord."[110]

Shortly after that announcement, Elizabeth conceives John, but at this time she keeps her pregnancy secret. So now when that same angel visits Mary, he gives her this news:

---

[110] Luke 1:15, 17 (LSB).

> "And behold, your relative Elizabeth has also conceived a son in her old age. And this is the sixth month for her who was called barren. For nothing will be impossible with God."[111]

So the first song that we're looking at today is Mary's response when she goes immediately after the annunciation to visit Elizabeth. And upon hearing Mary's greeting, what happens? The child in Elizabeth's womb, John, *leaps for joy*. This is what Mary said:

> "My soul magnifies the Lord,
> And my spirit has rejoiced in God my Savior.
> "For He has looked upon the humble state of His slave,
> For behold, from this time on, all generations will count me blessed.
> "For the Mighty One has done great things for me,
> And holy is His name.
> "AND HIS MERCY IS UPON GENERATION AFTER GENERATION
> TOWARD THOSE WHO FEAR HIM.
> "He has done a mighty deed with His arm;
> He has scattered those who were proud in the thoughts of their heart.
> "He has brought down rulers from their thrones,
> And has exalted those who were humble.
> "HE HAS FILLED THE HUNGRY WITH GOOD THINGS,
> And sent away the rich empty-handed.
> "He has given help to Israel His servant,
> In remembrance of His mercy,
> As He spoke to our fathers,

[111] Luke 1:36-37 (LSB).

> To Abraham and his seed forever."[112]

What a remarkable song of praise.

At this point we might ask, how do we know that music has always been a part of the praise of God in heaven and on earth? I'm glad you asked that. Because the earliest known song was sung by the angels at the very beginning of creation. And how do we know that? We read this in the 38th chapter of Job. After Job and his friends debate the nature of suffering for a good long while, God finally speaks up and questions Job and says this:

> "Where were you when I laid the foundation of the earth? . . .
> When the morning stars sang together
> And all the sons of God shouted for joy?"[113]

There was praise at the day of creation. In fact, we're told that *all* creation, even the inanimate creation, sings for joy. And if that's the case, then how much more would that be for the voice of men and of angels?

Psalm 96:12 says:

---

[112] Luke 1:46-55 (LSB).

[113] Job 38:4, 7 (LSB).

> Let the field exult, and all that is in it.
> Then all the trees of the forest will sing for joy.[114]

Psalm 98, verse eight, says:

> Let the rivers clap their hands,
> Let the mountains sing together for joy.[115]

Even nature sings the praises of God in a manner of speaking. Singing to God is not only a natural expression of worship, it's also a *command* for us to give God the praise that is due to his name. And even then, we could say it's for a very specific reason. Listen to what the prophet Zechariah says:

> "Sing for joy and be glad, O daughter of Zion; for behold, I am coming and I will dwell in your midst," declares Yahweh.[116]

The promise of God and the hope of his people is that God will dwell with them again as he once did in the Garden. And what is that name that is given to Jesus that reflects that reality? He's called *Immanuel, God with us*.

---

[114] Ps 96:12 (LSB).

[115] Ps 98:8 (LSB).

[116] Zec 2:10 (LSB).

Isaiah foretells the following mystery. In chapter seven, verse 14, he says:

> "Therefore the Lord Himself will give you a sign: Behold, the virgin will be with child and bear a son, and she will call His name Immanuel."[117]

God promises to come to us in human flesh and to dwell among his people. All this is foretold in the prophets and it is prefigured in what we call the Old Testament economy, the Tabernacle and the Temple. What was the point of that? It was building a tent for God to dwell in in the middle of the camp of his people. We have that idea, throughout the Old Testament, of God taking up residence with his people. So Mary now sings the praises of God who has purposed to fulfill this promise through her own body so that the child she bears will be called the Son of God.

Does Mary claim to deserve this honor? Or does she see herself as a kind of queen for bearing the child of the Most High? No. She refers to herself as *a slave girl*, a willing handmaiden of God to be used as he sees fit. She merely counts herself blessed to be used for this honor, but she never takes any glory to herself for this high calling. This song is not about her. It's about her *Savior*. So rather, she's looking to the promises that God has made to his people. They go back to Abraham 2,000 years, and then even further back than that, because the Seed that is promised, who will

[117] Is 7:14 (LSB).

crush the head of the serpent, is a promise given to Adam and Eve, way back in the Garden of Eden. So you see really from beginning to end, the story of the Bible has been the story about Christ through thousands of years of anticipation saying, *he's coming, he's coming*. And now announcing, *he's here, he's here*. So the anticipation of the ages is now upon this young woman, Mary, and she counts herself blessed to be used as the fulfillment. She shows that she knows her Bible and she expresses remarkable maturity and insight in this song of praise. She shows that she is indeed prepared to be used of God in fulfillment of his promises. We should remember as well that Mary was probably just a young woman, perhaps a teenager at this time. Now there's no pretense on her part. Mary never would have said, *oh, I knew it would be me*. She would never have said any such thing. In fact, it's a ridiculous myth to think that Mary herself is worthy of adoration when she herself expresses her confidence in God as her *savior*—that she will indeed be the human mother of Jesus, but he will be *her* savior as well.

Next we come to Zechariah's song. Since Zechariah disbelieved the message that Gabriel brought to him, he was struck dumb. He couldn't speak for the next number of months, maybe the better part of a year. Now, shortly after the birth of John, he got his voice back and he almost immediately broke out in a song of praise, speaking first about Jesus and then about his son, John. This is what he says in Luke chapter 1, starting in verse 67:

> And his father Zechariah was filled with the Holy Spirit, and prophesied, saying:
> "Blessed be the Lord God of Israel,
> For He visited and accomplished redemption for His people,
> And raised up a horn of salvation for us
> In the house of David His servant—
> As He spoke by the mouth of His holy prophets from of old—
> Salvation FROM OUR ENEMIES,
> And FROM THE HAND OF ALL WHO HATE US,
> To show mercy toward our fathers,
> And to remember His holy covenant,
> The oath which He swore to Abraham our father,
> To grant us that we, being rescued from the hand of our enemies,
> Might serve Him without fear,
> In holiness and righteousness before Him all our days.

And then Zechariah now addresses his son John:

> "And you, child, will be called the prophet of the Most High,
> For you will go on BEFORE THE LORD TO MAKE READY HIS WAYS,
> To give to His people the knowledge of salvation
> By the forgiveness of their sins,
> Because of the tender mercy of our God,
> With which the Sunrise from on high will visit us,
> TO SHINE UPON THOSE WHO SIT IN DARKNESS AND THE SHADOW OF DEATH,

To direct our feet into the way of peace."[118]

Like Mary, Zechariah sees the time of the fulfillment at hand. And his son John is now going to be the forerunner who will prepare the way for the coming King Jesus. He will be a herald of good news on the one hand, but he's also going to have a warning of judgment for those who remain in their sin. So God is bringing his covenant promises to pass in this generation. John is going to be that prophet who breaks the 400 year silence. He will be the last of the Old Testament prophets, each of whom in their own way foreshadowed the coming of the Messiah. And the Messiah is that, I'll call it capital-P, *Prophet* who was foretold in the scriptures, who is the full and the final revelation of God.

Isaiah pointed to this moment 600 years earlier. He says this in chapter 40:

> "Comfort, O comfort My people," says your God.
> "Speak to the heart of Jerusalem;
> And call out to her, that her warfare has been fulfilled,
> That her iniquity has been removed,
> That she has received from the hand of Yahweh
> Double for all her sins."
> A voice is calling,
> "Prepare the way for Yahweh in the wilderness;
> Make smooth in the desert a highway for our God.

[118] Luke 1:67-79 (LSB).

> "Let every valley be lifted up,
> And every mountain and hill be made low;
> And let the rough ground become a plain,
> And the rugged terrain a broad valley;
> Then the glory of Yahweh will be revealed,
> And all flesh will see it together;
> For the mouth of Yahweh has spoken."[119]

As I read that passage, I can hear the music from Handel's *Messiah* in my head because he used verses from that passage in Isaiah 40. In fact, he begins at the very beginning of this, he begins with that recitative, *comfort, comfort my people*. And then there's a chorus later on, *every valley shall be exalted*, right? These are words that find beautiful expression in song.

John is going to serve as the King's herald, the one who goes ahead of the King to prepare the way for the King, to make the highway smooth in anticipation of the King's arrival. What does that mean? It means the herald not only is announcing the arrival of the King, but frankly, making sure that nothing would get in his way. John's birth was the fulfillment of several specific Old Testament prophecies, one of which we quoted here from Isaiah, and another that was quoted by the angel.

---

[119] Is 40:1-5 (LSB).

Next that brings us to the angel's song. The anthem of the angels, as I might describe it, is like the glory of heaven springing a leak at this turning point in history. It's as if heaven cannot contain the good news of the arrival of the Christ child. So it must be announced—it's an *annunciation*. It must be accompanied by songs of praise. Angels are the heavenly choir of praise that have been glorifying God since they were created and they will continue throughout eternity. When we get a glimpse like this into heaven, we often see this very thing—that angels as well as saints together are singing the praises of God. By that, we might understand that when we sing together in a group like this, we're just warming up for that heavenly chorus.

Luke's narrative describes the scene in chapter two, starting in verse eight.

> In the same region there were some shepherds staying out in the fields and keeping watch over their flock by night. And an angel of the Lord stood before them, and the glory of the Lord shone around them; and they were terribly frightened. But the angel said to them, "Do not be afraid; for behold, I bring you good news of great joy which will be for all the people. For today in the city of David there has been born for you a Savior, who is Christ the Lord. And this will be the sign for you: you will find a baby wrapped in cloths and lying in a manger."

Here it comes:

> And suddenly there appeared with the angel a multitude of the heavenly host praising God and saying,
>
> "Glory to God in the highest,
> And on earth peace among men with whom He is pleased."[120]

With a little bit of reverent humor here, we could say that this was the very first Christmas concert. And what a choir that must have been! What a choir. At this moment, heaven is literally bursting with praise that spills over into the earth. We get a glimpse of the unseen reality of heavenly worship at this moment in time. No man ever heard such a choir than this, an army of God's angels singing praise to him to announce the birth of his beloved Son.

Notice how *light* is a recurring motif in the ministry of Christ. We see the light breaking forth here in the fields in the middle of the night. Later, there's going to be a heavenly light that will lead some pagan magicians from a distant land to come to worship the Christ child. We could go all the way back to the beginning and see that God revealed himself in the light at the very beginning of creation when he said, *let there be light*. And then we also think of how God gave a pillar of light to lead the Israelites through the desert for 40 years. Again, the angel song brings to mind a chorus from Handel's *Messiah*, which is one of the many settings of this

---

[120] Luke 2:8-14 (LSB).

text. It's an announcement of *good news*. I have to say *announcement* because we don't want to mistake it as a set of instructions for how to have a better life. We see it's a declaration of peace, which means that there was some kind of war or some kind of conflict before this moment. And we should not be wrapped in sentiment here. We should think of this like a diplomatic envoy that is dispatched into the enemy camp in order to declare terms of peace. It is an announcement of reconciliation to the party who caused the offense. That would be *us*. This Child will be the reconciliation of God with man. This Child is going to be the one who defeats the Serpent according to the promise of God to Adam and Eve.

The Latin setting for this text goes like this:

> *Gloria in excelsis Deo et in terra pax hominibus bonae voluntatis.*

You're going to recognize those first four words as a familiar refrain in many Christmas hymns: *Gloria in excelsis Deo.*

Finally, let's look at Simeon's song. This takes place shortly after the birth of Jesus, when he's brought into the Temple. In chapter two of Luke, starting in verse 25:

> And behold, there was a man in Jerusalem whose name was Simeon, and this man was righteous and devout, waiting for the comfort of Israel, and the Holy Spirit was upon him. And it had been revealed to him by the Holy Spirit that he would not see death before he had seen the Lord's Christ. And he came in the Spirit into the temple, and when the parents brought in the child Jesus to carry out for Him the custom of the Law, then he took Him into his arms and blessed God, and said,
>
> > "Now Master, You are releasing Your slave in peace,
> > According to Your word.
> > For my eyes have seen Your salvation,
> > Which You prepared in the presence of all peoples,
> > A LIGHT FOR REVELATION TO THE GENTILES,
> > And for the glory of Your people Israel."[121]

Christ will be a light to his people Israel *and* to the Gentiles—and that in fulfillment of the prophets. That's good news for those of us who are not descendants of Abraham—which probably includes most of the present company.

Isaiah said this in chapter 49, verses five and six:

> So now says Yahweh, who formed Me from the womb to be His Servant,
> To return Jacob back to Him, so that Israel might be gathered to Him
> (For I am glorified in the sight of Yahweh,
> And My God is My strength),

[121] Luke 2:25-32 (LSB).

> He says, "It is too small a thing that You should be My Servant
> To raise up the tribes of Jacob and to cause the preserved ones of Israel to return;
> I will also give You as a light of the nations
> So that My salvation may reach to the end of the earth."[122]

The Old Testament prophecies speak of salvation for the Gentiles over and over again. This is nothing new. We also notice that, going back to Abraham, the promise is not just for his descendants, but that through him, *all the nations of the earth will be blessed.*

Now what Simeon concluded in his statement has an ominous warning to it. I want to take a moment to consider this. In chapter two, verses 34 and 35:

> And Simeon blessed them and said to Mary His mother, "Behold, this Child is appointed for the fall and rise of many in Israel, and for a sign to be opposed—and a sword will pierce through your own soul as well—that the thoughts from many hearts may be revealed."[123]

And so it is today. Christ himself warned that his ministry was a ministry of *division*, that even the closest family relationships would be disrupted on account of him, that he leaves no one indifferent, but that men either

---

[122] Is 49:5-6 (LSB).

[123] Luke 2:34-35 (LSB).

come to him for salvation or they will be crushed by him like a boulder. As we saw in Psalm 2 sometime back, *those who will not kiss the Son will be crushed like a rod of iron crushes a clay pot*. So what do *you* think of this child? Does he bring you to a point of adoration or does he disgust you? Do you see him as the Savior of the world, even yourself who is a Gentile sinner? Or do you see him as a threat to the established religious and political order—a man worthy of death? Whatever the case, no one can be indifferent. Christ will either be your Lord and Savior, or he will be your righteous Judge. Don't be fooled by the sentimental idea that this baby Jesus is not the very same Creator and Judge of the world. He was the Creator of the world at the beginning, and he will be the Judge of the world at the end. He came into the world to save the world. He died and rose again to justify the wicked. Those who trust in him will not be put to shame, but he will come again in glory to judge both the living and the dead. So see to it that you put your trust in the one who has the power of an indestructible life, the Alpha and the Omega, the A and the Z, the beginning and the end of all things, the one who can give life to dry bones so that they live again, and live forever.

Although this season should be a happy time of the season for us, not everyone admittedly has fond memories of Christmas—especially at those times when we may be far removed from our friends and family. And those kinds of things are the consequences of sin, the things that separate us. But remember that the joy of the season is found in the assurance that Christ is the Light of the world and that he has come to save the world from the darkness and the despair of sin. So no matter what your circumstances, the songs of scripture and of our Christian tradition point us to a greater reality: the reason for hope for all men everywhere. The anticipation of the ages is accomplished in the birth of Christ. It's what we've been waiting for since God promised that the Seed of the woman would crush the head of the serpent.

I'm going to finish with three short quotations by Jesus from the book of John.

> Then Jesus again spoke to them saying, "I am the light of the world. He who follows me will never walk in the darkness, but will have the light of life."[124]
>
> "While I am in the world, I am the light of the world."[125]
>
> "For this reason, I have been born. And for this, I have come into the world to bear witness to the truth. Everyone who is of the truth hears my voice."[126]

---

[124] John 8:12 (LSB).

[125] John 9:5 (LSB).

[126] John 18:37c (LSB).

Jesus remains in the world today through his Word and through his Spirit. And he will soon come again in glory to judge the living and the dead. In the meantime, let us continue to sing his praises as we wait for that great day so that we can all say, *Gloria in Excelsis Deo*.

Amen.

Father, we thank you for this precious word and I pray that you would apply it to each and every one here. Help us to know the joy of the season, not in our own circumstances, but because of what Christ has accomplished for us in his life and death and resurrection. We pray these things in his name. Amen.

The Good Society (Psalm 128)

January 7, 2024

Today the text we're going to be looking at is Psalm 128.

Now this might be a little bit of a memory test. How many of you remember when we talked about Psalm 127? Don't feel badly if you don't remember. It was exactly a year ago when we covered the 127th Psalm. And I'm going to be reviewing that a little bit today because these two psalms fit together very nicely.

Let me read the 128th for you today.

1 How blessed is everyone who fears Yahweh,
Who walks in His ways.
2 When you shall eat of the fruit of the labor of your hands,
How blessed will you be and how well will it be for you.
3 Your wife shall be like a fruitful vine
In the innermost parts of your house,
Your children like olive plants
All around your table.
4 Behold, for thus shall the man be blessed
Who fears Yahweh.
5 May Yahweh bless you from Zion,
That you may see the prosperity of Jerusalem all the days of your life.

6 Indeed, may you see your children's children.
Peace be upon Israel![127]

Amen.

The title of the message today is *The Good Society*. The Good Society.

If I posed this question to you—tell me if you think it's an exaggeration—is our society falling apart in front of our eyes? Are we not seeing the chaos of our time? And why is that? If we could put a finger on it, what is it that is at the bottom of it? And this psalm is going to help us answer that question. Now, if you were to take these two psalms, 127, as well as 128, we could say that these two psalms, both very short, they pose a full frontal assault on our culture today. Because they crash headlong into the value system that we have embraced in our society at this particular point in history. And these two psalms help to show just how upside-down our values have become. This is a message that needs to be preached by the church, and it's a message that needs to be heard by a culture that's dying as we speak.

Why is it? What's going on in our culture? I could wax long about this, but let me summarize it by saying this: *we live in a narcissistic culture of*

[127] Ps 128 (LSB). Quoted again afterward.

incessant affirmation. The idea that whatever you come up with has to be *approved* and *encouraged* by everyone else in society, no matter how absurd it may be, and no matter how self-destructive it may be.

These two psalms taken together form a very interesting combination. Their arrangement in the Psalter next to each other is not accidental. So they can be understood in complementary fashion. And since it's been a year—and even the best of us probably need a little bit of a refresher—we're going to take just a moment to review Psalm 127 before we get into the text of 128.

If we were to identify the *theme* of Psalm 127, it is this recurring idea: *unless Yahweh . . . unless Yahweh*—that God has to be behind the plans of man and that man's plans must be in alignment with God in order to bring glory to him, or else the alternative is that everything that man does is *in vain*. It all comes to nothing. And this principle of the futility of work apart from God is never more true than it is in regard to the family. So Psalm 128 builds on the idea of God blessing man and blessing society through the godly family.

In Psalm 127, we're told that children are *an inheritance of Yahweh*. They are also a means of *defense* for the family—that specifically, children are a defense against those who would threaten the peace of the city. And that has a tie into the psalm we're looking at today because the very last petition in Psalm 128 is, *peace be upon Israel.* God has to be in the building of the home and the family. And we need to be reminded that children are *his* inheritance, and not ours.

In contrast to the blessings of work done in God's purposes, there is the futility of work that's done apart from God. And in this life, we often have to walk by faith and not by sight. We have to be willing to invest the time and energy according to God's word, not necessarily seeing all the results of our work, and even sometimes seeing the best of our work come to nothing.

Now in this psalm, we can say it's a very simple plan for the building of society, and it's presented to us in six very short verses. And yet this psalm, in spite of how brief it is, is deep enough to lay a foundation for all of society. And it's the foundation we need to be reminded of at this particular point in our history. It also illustrates how the wisdom of man is foolishness in God's sight. That all the clever innovations of man are pushed aside in order to show just how simple God's plan has been from the very beginning. This psalm can be understood by the simplest among us, and yet it could also be inexhaustible by the most sophisticated.

One of the themes that we see running through these two psalms, it's an implicit theme, and it's the theme of *love*. Now we don't think of these psalms as being love psalms, but they are in this sense, because it's describing, first of all, *the love of man for God*. It's also describing *the love of God for his people*. It's describing *the love that's expressed in the home*. It's describing *the love that's expressed between brethren in the church*. It's expressing *the love of one neighbor for another* in society. And it's describing a kind of love that our culture can scarcely comprehend, because it's a kind of love that has a lot more to do with *duties* than it has to do with *feelings*.

While the emphasis in these psalms is on *blessing*, we need to remember that when the Bible talks about blessing, there's something else in the background—that the opposite of the blessing is the *curse*. And so to fail to pay attention to what these psalms are saying about how to put yourself in the path of God's *blessing*, we need to be reminded that our failure to do that is asking for God's *judgment*. And indeed, I would argue that we are seeing the results of that right before our eyes.

Here are the five points that we want to cover in the six verses of this psalm. And I've come up with a method for hopefully making them a little more memorable for you. And think of this as starting from the inside out. So the first is a godly *man*. The second is a godly *marriage*. The third is a godly *mansion*, referring to the home. The fourth is a godly *ministry*, referring to the church. And lastly, a godly *metropolis*, referring to society. Part of the lesson should be that there is not going to be a shortcut to the good society. It has to start with the godly man, and from there it flows outward. We can think in terms of how a tiny stream may start as a trickle, but it grows into a great and mighty river.

First we'll consider *a godly man*. The first two verses:

> 1 How blessed is everyone who fears Yahweh,
> Who walks in His ways.
> 2 When you shall eat of the fruit of the labor of your hands,
> How blessed will you be and how well will it be for you.

The idea of fearing Yahweh is one that recurs frequently in scripture. What does that mean? We don't have to work very hard to answer that question because the first verse of this Psalm answers it for us, doesn't it? That is, the one *who walks in his ways*. Meaning what? Walking according to his *law*. Walking according to *obedience* to him. If we fear God and walk in his ways, then that means we don't have to fear man. We don't have to fear what man thinks about us or says about us. And we don't have to fear what man can do to us, either. As fallen people, it's a constant temptation for us to want to follow the crowd. But especially at a time like this, we should not be taking our cues from a society that is crumbling in front of our eyes. So if we fear Yahweh, we can say that we do not have to fear the one who destroys the body, that is, man. Because we *fear the one who can destroy both body and soul in hell*, just as Jesus warns us.

Next, we could say that we are to walk in his ways and conversely, *not* to walk in the way of the wicked. We don't have to guess what it means to fear Yahweh. It is God who defines what is right and wrong in his word, and it's also God who defines what it means to love. Truth comes from God's word. It does not—contrary to popular belief—it does *not* come from man's opinions. It does *not* come from any trend in culture or society. The outward result of an inner disposition that loves God is obedience to his commands. And this is often described as walking with him. So we can think of it in terms of a journey. And we constantly refer to the Christian *walk*, or the Christian *journey*, or the *pilgrimage* of the Christian life. The opposite is also in view, just as it is elsewhere in scripture, that we *do not* walk in the way of the wicked and we should *not* be drawn into his wicked works. God's path is the path of life and blessing, whereas the wicked walk in the path of destruction.

Next, we're told that we should work with our hands. We are to be *productive*. Diligence in our labor is part of God's purpose for man from the very beginning. This is part of the way that man exercises dominion over God's creation. Man's labor brings glory to his creator, and it also provides what man needs to live and to thrive on the earth. If there's a *command*, then there's also a *prohibition* behind it, as in this case. So if we're told to work with our hands and to work diligently, then we could also think of passages such as in Proverbs, where it warns us repeatedly not to be like the sluggard. Every man has an individual responsibility to provide for himself first of all, and also to help those who are in need. The scripture tells us to *redeem the time for the days are evil*, that *we are to work while it is day*. Labor is to be a lifelong endeavor for us, and we're reminded throughout that effort matters, both in terms of our physical labor as well as in terms of our spiritual labor. We have passages that say, for example, *whatever your hand finds to do, to do it with all your might*. We're also told that we are to *run the race in order to win*, to compete as if there is only one prize. Even the Great Commandment reflects the imperative of what we could call a total effort, doesn't it? That we are to *love the Lord our God with all of our heart, soul, mind, and strength*.

Life is not merely about labor. There is a blessing that comes from that labor. We have the opportunity to enjoy the produce of our work. So there's a time and a season for work, and we're to work diligently, but God also sets aside times for us to rest. And not only to rest, but also to take enjoyment in that rest as we make use of those things that our work has provided. Our rest is most profitable when we use it to reflect on God's blessings for us, as we do particularly on the Lord's Day. We are to find contentment in the things that he has provided through the work of our hands. Blessedness describes the condition of being under God's favor. But here's the warning: it doesn't necessarily mean that life is always going to be easy. We're told even from Genesis 3 onward that life is going to be toilsome. It's going to require effort and sweat and hardship. Adam is told to toil by the sweat of his brow. And we also notice that he's warned that some of his effort is going to end up being wasted on things like thorns and thistles. He's going to have to fight against those kinds of things, even as he toils to bring forth bread from the ground. So that should lead us to say that there are going to be times when we may suffer loss in this life, in spite of our most diligent labor. And when that happens—and we think of Job as the case of someone for whom it happened to a great measure—we should be reminded that our temporal effort comes with an eternal reward, that it's not just about building up what we need on earth for food and for provision, but also building treasures in heaven. God never fails to account for our labor. So that first part, that's all about the godly man, the one who seeks God and who pursues him walking in his ways.

Next, *a godly marriage*—marriage by God's design. Verse three:

> 3 Your wife shall be like a fruitful vine
> In the innermost parts of your house,

> Your children like olive plants
> All around your table.

We're reminded in Psalm 127 that children are *like arrows in the quiver of a warrior*. So we have these word pictures that are given to us about the value of children. Now, it's not very popular to say this. If anybody is offended and needs to leave, I'll understand. But marriage is to be between one man and one woman for a lifetime. And no other relationship fits the definition of marriage. And not only that, but man does not have any authority to redefine marriage because it is God's institution. And it's not just that marriage is important, or that it comes first. We have to understand that marriage is the most *fundamental*, the most *important*, and the most *powerful* institution in society. That without marriage, we have nothing else. It is like the building block that we build from. And if we have bricks of sand rather than stone, we have nothing to build with. Without marriage, society becomes impossible. You cannot build a society without it, and a society that has been built on marriage cannot be sustained for very long without it. If we have the attitude that marriage is just a piece of paper, then it really does become worthless. And it's worthless because, as one philosopher said, you can write anything on a piece of paper.

All sorts of people can marry, but there's a special requirement for those who are Christians to marry *only in the Lord*, only to marry another

Christian. And the violation of that particular restriction has been the cause of countless broken homes and considerable misery. We're commanded not to be *unequally yoked*. And Paul asks this kind of rhetorical question, *what fellowship does Christ have with Belial?* In other words, a marriage between a Christian and unbeliever is like trying to form a spiritual union between Christ and the Devil. It's simply not possible. Marriage is not designed to be a way to rescue the lost. We're to marry only in Christ.

Next—also not very popular—that love involves *actions* more than *feelings*. Husbands are commanded to love their wives as Christ loved the church, which means to provide for and to protect their wives. Wives are commanded to respect their husbands whom God gives for both physical and spiritual care. And wives should be reminded that the husband is an office holder whose position commands respect because he carries the responsibility for the care of his family. And God will judge him on that basis.

Next—this is also not very popular—and that is to *be fruitful* in the field and in the home. Something that's interesting to notice from the very beginning, what we see in Adam and Eve is that Adam is given chiefly to the labor of the *field* and that Eve is given chiefly to the labor of the *home*. So this admonition is in view: that women need to stop trying to prove that they can be like men by rejecting what it means to be a woman. God has made her to be a helper to her husband, not a substitute. And true feminism means being the woman that God made you to be, not being something else. Now, men likewise need to be men and not girls. They are to protect and to provide for their families, even to the point of laying down their own lives if necessary. Trying to reverse those God-given roles of husband and wife in marriage is a formula for failure because it goes against the nature of marriage itself. We could say that it's as foolish as trying to defy the laws of gravity.

Next, regarding children. They're to be submissive to their parents and they're to be trained in virtue. Parents are to be parents and not taxi drivers. No one else can love children as the parents do, which makes it very foolish to put them into someone else's care. In the book of Proverbs, we have admonitions like this, to *train up a child in the way he should go, so that when he is old, he will not depart from it*. In the book of Ephesians, when talking about the order of the home, Paul specifically addresses the children and says to *obey your parents in the Lord, for this is right*. And he also says to fathers, *do not provoke your children*. We are reminded in the law that the promises that God has given to his people are not only for us, but for our children—and we have a solemn duty to teach them everything that God commands. You could ask the question like this. If we're evangelistic in our mind, where does the Great Commission start if it doesn't start in the home? So your family is the first place for mission work.

Social order also begins in the home. In other words, a structure of leadership and submission. And if we don't find that kind of order in the home, we frankly shouldn't expect to find it anywhere else. God ordains all the structures in society that we are to live and to work within. And that begins in the home. There's never any justification for thinking that God intends for men to simply do their own thing without any kind of external social order, or to think that their personal choices don't have an effect on anyone else.

I'm going to continue with the theme of unpopular topics by saying something about divorce now—that *God hates divorce*, especially when it's done for selfish reasons. So I'll only speak briefly about this and think about these three things. First of all, that the Bible does permit divorce in a few specific circumstances where the sin has been egregious and where reconciliation has failed. But secondly, most divorce that occurs today is frivolous and it's therefore sinful. Because your particular feelings of the moment are not the basis for deciding whether to continue or dissolve the marriage. Thirdly, I have to add, for the sake of the children, that it's a lie to suggest that divorce is better for the children than keeping an intact family. And this is frankly how selfish parents try to justify their decision to break a relationship that is meant to last for a lifetime. And part of the reason that relationship is meant for a lifetime is for the benefit of the children in the home.

Lastly, I want to address in this section, a fallacy of inequality because marriage does not make men, women, and children unequal, nor does any other institution in society. And this is one of the most destructive fallacies of the modern era. It is used by opponents of marriage to destroy God's institution by trying to turn it into a kind of slavery, which it is not. Marriage provides structure so that we can glorify God in our various callings and according to our various gifts. It is to be a place of refuge and not a prison camp. The reason why this is so important is because *marriage is the pattern for every other social institution*. That's why we're talking about it first. If we do not have marriage as a foundation for society, there would be no order in any other part of society.

The next section has to do with *a godly mansion*. And here I'm referring to the home—domestic life, the labors of home and family. So this verse—verse four—is very closely connected to the one that we just looked at.

> 4 Behold, for thus shall the man be blessed
> Who fears Yahweh.

It is a command from the very beginning of the Bible for us to *be fruitful and multiply*. It's a command that's first given to the whole creation. And it is the reason why God created life in the first place. And no form of life is more precious in God's sight than human life. Because man is his most special creation. We say that man is made *in the image of God*. That man has a special relationship with his Creator that is not found anywhere else in the creation. And God gives us the ability and the privilege of being part of his creative work.

We could also talk about the importance of a division of labor, because we see this from the very beginning. It's first of all reflected in the complementary nature of marriage itself: men laboring in the field to bring forth *the fruit of the ground*, and women laboring in the home to bring forth *the fruit of the womb*. There are also complementary results, because think about this: we saw in Psalm 127 that the point of building a house is so that you can put a family in it. So that labor in the field provides what is needed for the labor in the home. And labor provides for one's needs, but it's also intended for higher ends.

Care is designed to begin in the home as well. Parents caring for their children, grown children caring for their aging parents. And there's a very stern warning in the Apostle Paul, in his writings: it says that *those who do not care for the members of their own household have denied the faith and they become worse than unbelievers*. So God intends for family to be that place for caring both for the young and for the aged. God is most glorified when we fulfill the purposes he has made us for. So that we can say in this verse, *thus the man shall be blessed who fears Yahweh.*

Next, let's think about *a godly ministry*. We're starting from the individual. We've talked about the individual *man*, then the *marriage*, now the *home*. Now we can go out to the next step, which is the life of the *church*. Verse five:

> 5 May Yahweh bless you from Zion,
> That you may see the prosperity of Jerusalem all the days of your life.

Of course, the corollary to work is *rest*. There are times of work and rest, and one of the most important things that we do during our rest is to praise and give thanks to God for the blessings that he's given us. Our highest end is to glorify him and to enjoy him both in this life and in the next. And while that physical labor is of some profit for the present life, we should not fail to be laboring for eternal treasures as well. So no matter how much you have in this life, the warning is that you have to leave it all behind when you leave.

Just as there has to be order in the family, there's also order in the church. We have the picture of *shepherds* who are overseeing the *flock*. That means that there are those who have *authority* in the church to care for those who are the *members* of the church. And there's a very strong parallel here in the church as with the family. In fact, we could say that the church is like an extended family. It is even called *the household of God*. We also notice that when Paul is laying out the requirements for church leadership, what does he say? That *if you haven't managed your own home well, then how are you going to care for the household of* God? So leadership starts in the home.

In the church, we have the priority of corporate worship when we come together on the Lord's Day for worship. It's certainly profitable for us to worship in our families, but there are some elements of worship that are reserved for the church under the authority of the officers in the church. So that relationship to the church is not to be neglected. It's also where we show love for the brethren, where we share our gifts and our graces. And that is for the purpose of building up one another, edifying one another in our Christian lives. Paul talks about *varieties of gifts*. And the reason why there are varieties of *gifts* is because there are varieties of *needs*. And so, each one sharing his gift according to someone's need. Also in the church, we have both *teaching* and *accountability*. One of the most important responsibilities of those who are given leadership in the home and in the church is teaching. Discipleship means *learning*. If there are *students*, then that means there have to be *teachers*. And teachers have a solemn responsibility to teach what accords with the *truth*, and not just the parts they like best, but to teach *all* of it. And it never matters whether truth is popular or not. In fact, we shouldn't be surprised to say that most of the time truth is not popular, but we have to teach it anyway.

Lastly—we're working our way out from the *home*, and now from the *church* into the *community*. So this is *a godly metropolis*, a godly *city* or a godly *nation*. Verse six:

> 6 Indeed, may you see your children's children. . . .

And then this last statement:

> Peace be upon Israel!

As individuals and families and churches, we have a command to love our neighbors. That means helping those who are in need. It also means discipling those who do not know Christ. When we think about the role of government, good government involves those who understand that they are servants of God, who use their authority to restrain evil in society. They are to carry out justice with integrity. The corollary is that they must never show partiality. They must never take bribes to pervert justice. Government is there to provide for the common good by maintaining civil order. But there's a limit to that because the exercise of authority should not infringe on the freedom that individuals have to care for themselves, to care for their families, and to care for their communities, as well as their duty to worship God in their churches.

Think about it this way: the good society does not need very much government. Why? Because government starts with the self. That was our first point. If we do not have godly *men*, we are not going to have godly *marriages*, or godly *homes*, or godly *churches*, or godly *societies*. And the warning here is that men should not look to the state for those things that God has ordained for the family, for the church, and for the community.

As we think about the role of the city or the metropolis, let me come back to the family. We have to think of the family as an *investment* in society. If you want to enjoy the blessings of a good society, you have to invest in a family, a strong family. And the payback of a stable *family* is then a stable *community* to live and work in. So there's this feedback loop that occurs when our families are strong, we can build strong churches, strong communities, and that gives us the ability to continue to build families. Think of it like bricks in a building. If the bricks begin to crumble, then we know the walls are soon going to collapse.

Another role that Christian families play in society is preservative in nature. In other words, having a godly family *in* society helps restrain God's judgment *against* society. This is part of what we understand by the idea that we are to be *salt and light* in our societies.

So we covered these five points in this little psalm. I bet you didn't think we could get that much out of it. We talked about the importance of *a godly man*, who forms *a godly marriage*, who builds *a godly mansion*, who is part of *a godly ministry*. And from there, he builds *a godly metropolis* or a godly society.

We really have just two choices in front of us. We can either fear God and follow his commandments or we can choose the path of self-destruction. We can seek God's mercy or we can suffer his judgment. He is longsuffering because he takes no pleasure in the death of the wicked, but that is not a license for sin. We should be reminded that *today is the day of salvation*, that it may be that *tonight your life is required of you*. And I always think of what happened in the days of Jonah when he went to preach to that great city Nineveh. And the message is what? *You have* 40 *days and Nineveh will be destroyed*, or *overthrown*. And what is the king's response when he hears that message? It's remarkable. He says, *who knows? God may turn and relent and turn from his fierce anger so that we may not perish*. And he sent out the command throughout the city for a fast, for a time of prayer and repentance. That is precisely what we need to do as a society in our own day.

Virtue has to begin with the individual who's committed to Christ. And anyone who seeks to change the values or the direction of society needs to start, first of all, with himself. And it is the gospel of Christ that has the power to transform the heart from a heart of stone to a heart of flesh.

From our message today, it should be easy to see that your most important part in building a better society is strengthening your own family. And it's never too late to start. That's the good news.

I would remind you that God was able to build society, first of all, from one marriage in the beginning between Adam and Eve, and then to rebuild society after the Flood from a single family. All it ever takes is one committed marriage.

I'm going to let Matthew Henry summarize these two Psalms for us today. Referring to Psalm 127, he says, in that one, "we were taught that the prosperity of our families depends upon the blessing of God." And then referring to Psalm 128, "in this, we are taught that the only way to obtain that blessing, which will make our families comfortable, is to live in the fear of God and in obedience to him."

Amen.

Let's pray. Father, this is a powerful word that you give to us today in these short verses. We pray that you would give us wisdom and understanding and hearts that truly long for you and seek to walk according to your ways all the days of our lives. Help us to build godly marriages, godly families, godly churches, and godly communities by seeking you and following after you all the days of our life. In Christ's name we pray. Amen.

Suggested Memory Verses

The Psalms are a rich source of encouragement and spiritual wisdom for the saint. The following verses are some of my favorites, and they are commended here for your memorization. Each verse by itself may prove to be a "life preserver" in time of trouble—when all other words fail. The suggested verses from Luke complement our studies in the Psalms and beautifully express—along with them—*The Music of the Gospel*.

May God bless your studies in his word!

Psalm 2

11 Serve Yahweh with fear
And rejoice with trembling. (LSB)

Psalm 14

6 You would put to shame the counsel of the afflicted,
But Yahweh is his refuge.
7 Oh, that the salvation of Israel would come out of Zion!
When Yahweh restores His captive people,
May Jacob rejoice, may Israel be glad. (LSB)

Psalm 19

14 Let the words of my mouth and the meditation of my heart
Be acceptable in Your sight,
O Yahweh, my rock and my Redeemer. (LSB)

Psalm 23

6 Surely goodness and mercy shall follow me all the days of
my life: and I will dwell in the house of the LORD for ever.
(KJV)

Psalm 34

18 Yahweh is near to the brokenhearted
And saves those who are crushed in spirit. (LSB)

Psalm 36

5 Your steadfast love, O LORD, extends to the heavens,
your faithfulness to the clouds. (ESV)

Psalm 46

1 God is our refuge and strength,
A very present help in trouble. (LSB)

Psalm 49

5 Why should I fear in days of evil,
When the iniquity of my supplanters surrounds me,
6 Even those who trust in their wealth
And boast in the abundance of their riches? (LSB)

Psalm 94

14 For Yahweh will not abandon His people,
Nor will He forsake His inheritance. (LSB)

19 When my anxious thoughts multiply within me,
Your consolations delight my soul. (LSB)

Psalm 110

1 Yahweh says to my Lord [Jesus]:
"Sit at My right hand
Until I put Your enemies as a footstool for Your feet." (LSB)

Psalm 127

1 Unless Yahweh builds the house,
They labor in vain who build it;
Unless Yahweh watches the city,
The watchman keeps awake in vain. (LSB)

Psalm 128

1 How blessed is everyone who fears Yahweh,
Who walks in His ways. (LSB)

Psalm 146

2 I will praise Yahweh throughout my life;
I will sing praises to my God while I have my being.
3 Do not trust in nobles,
In merely a son of man, in whom there is no salvation. (LSB)

Luke

1:49 For the Mighty One has done great things for me, and holy is His name. And His mercy is upon generation after generation toward those who fear Him. (LSB)

2:10-11 But the angel said to them, "Do not be afraid for behold, I bring you good news of great joy, which will be for all the people. For today in the city of David, there has been born for you a savior who is Christ the Lord." (LSB)

Bibliography

The following resources were used at various times in the preparation of these messages.

Commentaries:

Boice, J.M. *Psalms*. Three Volumes. Baker Books, Grand Rapids, Michigan. 1994.

Davidson, F., Stibbs, A.M., and Kevan, E.F., eds. *The New Bible Commentary*. W.B. Eerdmans Publishing Company, Grand Rapids, Michigan. Second Edition. 1965.

Dummelow, J.R., ed. *A Commentary on the Holy Bible by Various Writers*. MacMillan Publishing Company, New York, New York. 1908.

Church, L.F., ed. *Matthew Henry's Commentary in One Volume*. Zondervan, Grand Rapids, Michigan. 1961.

Henry, M., and Scott, T. *Logos Commentary on the Holy Bible: Job to Song of Solomon* (Volume 2). Logos International, Plainfield, New Jersey. Hardcover edition, n.d.

Kretzmann, P.E. *Popular Commentary of the Bible: Old Testament Volume II: The Poetical and Prophetic Books*. Concordia Publishing House, St. Louis, Missouri. 1924.

Leupold, H.C. *Exposition of the Psalms*. Baker Book House, Grand Rapids, Michigan. 1969.

Scroggie, W.G. *The Psalms*. Pickering & Inglis Ltd., London, England. 1965.

Spurgeon, C.H. *The Treasury of David*. Three Volumes. MacDonald Publishing Company, McLean, Virginia. Hardcover edition, n.d.

Study Bibles:

Harper Study Bible, Revised Standard Version. H. Lindsell, ed. Zondervan Bible Publishers, Grand Rapids, Michigan. 1971.

The MacArthur Study Bible, New King James Version. J. MacArthur, ed. Thomas Nelson, Nashville, Tennessee. 1997.

The NIV Study Bible, Tenth Anniversary Edition. K. Barker, ed. Zondervan Publishing House, Grand Rapids, Michigan. 1995.

The Reformation Study Bible, English Standard Version. R.C. Sproul, ed. Ligonier Ministries, Orlando, Florida. 2005.

Online Resources:

Blue Letter Bible (*www.blueletterbible.org*): "Blue Letter Bible provides powerful tools for an in-depth study of God's Word through our free online reference library, with study tools that are grounded in the historical, conservative Christian faith."

Sermon Audio (*www.sermonaudio.com/jrdickens*): "The largest and most trusted library of audio sermons from conservative churches and ministries worldwide."

About J.R. Dickens

J.R. Dickens holds a Ph.D. in mechanical engineering and has frequently served as a lay teacher in the church over the course of more than twenty years. His most extensive teaching topics include the book of Genesis, biblical creation, apologetics, and the Westminster Confession of Faith.

J.R. is the author of the *Coffee Talk* series of short books on Christian apologetics, as well as a timely booklet on the importance of recovering ecclesiastical authority. He recently published *Doctrines in Genesis* from a set of lectures delivered for a Reformation conference in 2021.

In the spring of 2023, J.R. was invited to teach *The Apologetics of Francis Schaeffer* at New Geneva Theological Seminary in Colorado Springs, Colorado, where he served two years as librarian for a collection of 25,000 printed titles.

J.R.'s personal interests include aviation, where he holds a commercial pilot certificate, instrument rating, and flight instructor rating. He also enjoys camping, hiking, and skiing.

The title of this volume is inspired by J.R.'s musical training, which includes many years playing the French horn (both band and orchestra) and numerous attempts at classical piano. He has written several original hymns.

J.R. can be reached by email at *jrdickens90@gmail.com*. His books are available on Amazon. Many of his messages can be heard on SermonAudio.

www.ingramcontent.com/pod-product-compliance
Lightning Source LLC
LaVergne TN
LVHW020701110826
845149LV00012B/2065